# THE V
## BUSINESS GUIDE

# THE VIRGIN INTERNET BUSINESS GUIDE

## VERSION 1.0

by Simon Collin

This edition first published in 2000 by
Virgin Publishing Ltd
Thames Wharf Studios
Rainville Road
London
W6 9HA

First published in Great Britain in 2000 by Virgin Publishing Ltd

Version 1.0 – July 2000

A catalogue record for this book is available from the British Library.

ISBN 0 7535 0463 4

Designed and typeset by John and Orna Designs, London
Printed and bound by Omnia Books Ltd, Glasgow

# //GET DOWN TO SOME SERIOUS BUSINESS

The Internet has changed the way in which every company carries out its business. The fundamental model that's been used for almost every business plan for the past dozen years has been thrown out and changed for a new net-based example that has cut-price web-based technology at its core. The web has already changed the way in which we expect to carry out our personal business – from managing our bank accounts to applying for a car loan – so it's hardly surprising that the business model, too, has changed.

To begin with, you can research and buy a company or franchise online, then improve your management skills with online training courses, before you take the business public with web-based venture capital and marketing consultants. Alternatively, why not improve your existing company with new methods that help cut costs and improve efficiency for marketing, fulfilment and banking?

In this book, we explain how to make the most of your business within the digital world and how to improve your arsenal of marketing, financial and management techniques using advice from gurus who are willing to supply their knowledge free, online. Alternatively, branch out and set up your own e-commerce site using the advice in Chapter 4; we tell you how to promote and sell goods and services cheaply and effectively online.

The Internet has only been open to commerce for the past few years, so it's a brave new world that's open to entrepreneurs. This book helps you make the most of the opportunities available and tells you how to adapt your business to make the most of the new business age, where everything starts with 'e'.

Simon Collin, who compiled this guide, is a technology writer and net-obsessive who has worked for many of the leading computer magazines and has written over two dozen books about computing and the Internet.

**Contact us**
The Internet is evolving so fast that, even though this book was correct at the time of going to press, there could be a few dud addresses or omissions. If you have any problems with anything in this book, send us an email at response@virgin-pub.co.uk. We'll make sure it's dealt with in the next edition.

# //CONTENTS

# 1//BUSINESS ON THE INTERNET

Reach a global audience, get advice, sell stuff, buy equipment, find import or export partners, make contacts, seek advice, recruit people, improve your marketing or search for new premises. That's the promise of using the Internet within your business – and we'll explain just how to take advantage of it all over the following chapters.

Like the telegraph and telephone before it, the Internet has totally turned the traditional business model on its head. It has, in the past couple of years, transformed the way businesses work, trade and interact. It's slashed costs, brought instant riches, turned tiny start-ups into international monsters – and all at an unbelievable speed. If you want to keep up with your competitors, create a new channel for your products, access a vast library, or simply improve productivity, then you should get online as soon as possible. The net's no longer a business luxury or the preserve of teenage hackers. It's an invaluable business tool that you need to use in order to work and compete in the future.

Thanks to the Internet, you can now set up a shop online just as easily as huge corporations – with just as much chance of success. It's levelled the pitch to give small companies the same chances and resources as the big guys. You can get instant – and often free – access to company reports, government briefings, export documents, travel information, management theories and just about every type of business adviser.

But perhaps the biggest revolution is just starting to catch on. Instead of targeting consumers, companies are now using the net for business-to-business transactions – to get prices, find a partner, interact, sign deals and even pay for machinery over the web.

## //WHAT CAN I DO?

There's a vast range of business-related resources on the web. Here are just some of the things you can do:

- get quotes for a new marketing campaign
- sell off old inventory
- bid for new machinery
- manage cashflow with access to your bank account
- find the best rates or cheapest deal for a loan
- pay bills
- get the latest financial news
- keep up with trade news from your niche area
- market your products more effectively
- buy a mailing list
- target a new, worldwide customer base
- sell products with little overheads
- discuss your business strategy
- get advice on any aspect of business.

The Internet was conceived as a tool for academics. In fact, commerce was banned from it until recently. Consumers, rather than business users, took over the web and have spent the past couple of years driving up shopping and entertainment websites and forcing the technical wizards to come up with the programs and methods needed to pay for goods and carry out a range of transactions. But now it's the turn of business to make use of the Internet. Up till now, the net has been at its best when distributing advice, news and information, but the new buzz is business-to-business (or B2B), and the pundits predict that inter-business trading over the net – buying machines, components, expertise – will easily outstrip online consumer spending.

You can already use the web to get bids from competing suppliers, find new advisers or enter an auction to buy or sell surplus stock. But if you're not quite ready to ditch your existing suppliers and contacts, the net is still packed with advice, ideas and tools to help manage, expand, export and market your business.

There are thousands of guides available: some are tucked away on company websites, as a service to their customers; others are gathered together on vast financial sites that try to cover all subjects, from export policies to e-commerce start-ups.

You can access research and analysis from the biggest and most influential world organisations – from your country's government to the World Bank. Add to this newspaper and magazine archives and you have a vast library of material that you can dip into anytime for ideas, answers and advice. Forget its history as an academic tool; the new breed of website has a mission to present information, techniques and economic theory in a way that's clear and accessible to everyone.

### Starting points
To get a flavour of the wide range of business sites that are on the net, here are ten great sites to try out before you leap in.

### 1 Financial Times                    www.ft.com
Keep up to date with concise, authoritative reporting on every aspect of business, finance and commerce.

### 2 OnVia                              www.onvia.com
Lets you request bids from online suppliers for just about anything, from new machines to mailing catalogues. Fantastic idea provides a view of the future of business.

### 3 Fast Company
www.fastcompany.com
The magazine that describes (and often defines) the perfect, cool and trendy new-world business model.

### 4 British Council
www.britcoun.org
Provides stacks of guides to help (primarily UK) businesses target new countries for export potential.

### 5 SurplusBin
www.surplusbin.com
Sell off your excess merchandise – or buy stock cheap. A fast, efficient way to get the market price without too much fuss and bother.

### 6 Greenfield Online
www.greenfield.com
The future of business market research? Maybe. Provides near-instant feedback from controlled user groups to market-test ideas, concepts and projects, saving time and money.

### 7 X-drive
www.xdrive.com
Forget the bar or photocopier room, this is the new place to share information, a diary, contacts, or gossip with colleagues.

### 8 Yahoo! Store
http://store.yahoo.com
Not the cheapest, nor the most flexible, but it'll let you set up a shop online with little programming expertise and promote it to the millions that visit Yahoo! – still the most popular site on the web.

### 9 GovWorks
www.govworks.com
The future direction of how business and government will interact. Find the US government department that does what you need, then talk directly via the web. Pay your bills or query policy and get answers.

### 10 Dialog
www.dialog.com
Astonishing depth of information thanks to the merger of MAID and Knight-Ridder's company information services. Just about all the business, legal, corporate and company news you could want.

## //THE WAY THE INTERNET WORKS

Before we look at how you can use the Internet in your business, let's start with some basic facts. If you're not online yet, turn to Chapter 2, or get up to speed on the basics of surfing with a copy of this book's sister volume, *The Virgin Guide to the Internet*.

Many people don't realise that the Internet is just a communications network – like a vast and technically sophisticated telephone system – designed to move data in the form of digital computer code around the planet. There are three major different systems on this network, and they each offer very different facilities, benefits and features to the consumer.

First, there's the World Wide Web (the web), which has a vast store of information that you can search out and read. Some information (such as share prices) is constantly renewed and delivered instantly on request. Other information, for example business advice or export guides, is like a magazine or news feature, except it is published electronically instead of on paper.

Second, there's electronic mail (email), which uses the net to send and receive messages; once you've installed email in your company, you'll never be able to look the fax machine in the eye again – it will totally change the way in which you communicate with your customers, suppliers and staff.

Third, there are discussion forums and newsgroups, in which you can talk to other people within a public forum. For some of these discussion groups you'll need to use a special software tool (called a newsgroup reader), but many are part of online magazine or newspaper sites where you can chat till you've had enough of typing. In the rest of this book, you'll see how all three of these features work together.

### Business goes online

The Internet was originally developed in the 1960s and 1970s for academic, military and government purposes. The early developers expected their network to be limited to a single group of organisations, such as the university world or national government offices. Most of their effort went into developing a 'resilient' network – one that could continue to work even if part of it was knocked out. The usual example is if it was damaged by a nuclear strike in the Cold War. They weren't too worried about the needs of the ordinary consumer, business, security, or speed. In fact, almost all businesses were banned from using the net (unless they were selected computer research firms). And it was only in the 1990s that business and trade started to appear on the net, greeted by loud complaints from the academics.

As the Internet started to gain in popularity, many computer companies were still highly sceptical about its use as a business tool. Even software giant Microsoft dismissed the net as a fad and for six months did little development for this new communications system. Six months later, it made a dramatic U-turn and set up vast development teams to work on Internet software. In common with its rivals, Microsoft was working to produce business software that helped make the net a safer, more reliable, and user-friendly place where businesses would feel comfortable surfing, selling and trading. It's taken a few years, but the web is now a safe, stable platform for business. In fact, the net is such an efficient, useful platform that it's forced almost every company to rethink their business model and basic strategy.

This impact has been felt on the stock markets, where the value of traditional manufacturing companies and chains of shops has dropped as virtual e-companies – those with no assets (or profits) except a domain name and slick website – have rocketed to astonishing levels. For example, the vast US bookseller Barnes and Noble (**www.bn.com**) owns hundreds of prime retail outlets but is dwarfed in value by Amazon.com (**www.amazon.com**), which also sells books but has no shop-based assets, a lower turnover and, at the time of writing, has yet to make a profit.

In the early days of the new business model, it seemed that a zany, memorable domain name and a slick website packed with interesting content counted for more than a real product, real shops, real profits. But today it is clear that the companies that will succeed in the long run are those that offer something original and use the Internet as another marketing channel. For example, magazines and newspapers have teams of journalists working to write news stories and features. Companies such as the Financial Times (**www.ft.com**) publish material on the web as well as in a daily newspaper. The FT is using the Internet as a new medium but, because it creates original content that its readers want, it will always be in a strong position.

Compare this with the plight of travel agents; online travel agents can do the same job as those based in high-street shops, but they have very low overheads (much lower rent and few staff). Both are simply sales and marketing outlets for someone else's products; if competition continues, the high-street shops could eventually disappear. And the online travel sites will only be able to keep customers by offering cut-price deals. The consumer and the original suppliers (the airlines, hotels and hire companies) are the winners; the loser is the middleman whose margins are squeezed by the efficiency of content delivery by the net.

## //CHANGING YOUR BUSINESS

To get the most from the Internet, you should examine the ways it can help you to be more efficient in every department or part of your business. Take marketing: where the Internet has added a whole new dimension to the way in which products can be promoted and sold. Direct marketing to consumers is still essential, but now it can be more efficient, faster and sent directly to a customer's desk. Press relations are just as important as ever, but you can use a specialist web-based agency to deliver press releases to thousands of journalists over the web. And thanks to those little rectangles of prime screen real estate called banner ads, new types of advertising have arrived. Of course, it's not as simple as this and there are plenty of limitations – a quick visit to the sites of the major traditional postal services, such as the Royal Mail (www.royalmail.co.uk), soon puts a different spin on the story.

Internet marketing not only provides a new opportunity, but also a whole stack of new techniques that are faster, more efficient and a lot cheaper than traditional methods. The net has provided a great way for small companies to match the big corporates on spread and reach – without having to rely on vast budgets. In Chapter 5, we cover all the main techniques used to market your traditional products and the more specialist requirements of marketing your new website.

The net has had a similar effect on the process of selling goods and services – by creating new ways to take orders and money from the customers. Just about every company is wondering how to set up a shop on the net and reach this vast new audience. Setting up a shop online is, technically, still one of the more difficult jobs for a web designer and developer. However, it's getting easier every day and, if you are prepared to outsource your shop, there are solutions from VirginBiz (www.virginbiz.net), Yahoo! (http://store.yahoo.com) and many other suppliers, such as iCat (www.icat.com), that promise to help you get your online shop up and running, with no technical expertise required, within a day.

The attractions of e-commerce are undeniable. Once the initial development costs have been met, often out of the marketing budget for the overall website, the online shop has a tiny monthly rent, low overheads, few additional staffing costs and, best of all, is open 24 hours per day to suit any potential international customer. Of course, you'll also have to consider order fulfilment and customer service. We cover all the equipment and techniques you'll need to set up and run a shop in Chapter 4.

A less dramatic way of making use of the Internet is to use it to help with your everyday financial transactions. You can check your bank balance, settle corporation tax or phone bills, pay for office furniture or order stationery online from thousands of websites. With all these sites, the most popular, convenient and safe way of paying for stuff on the net is to use a credit card. However, there are dozens of different ways to handle and spend your company's money; if you want the latest news on what's happening in online payment, visit CommerceNet (**www.commerce.com**).

You can organise regular payments, such as utility bills or even the company payroll, to be outsourced to specialist web-based companies, then tie the reported information back to your accounting software – unless you've also outsourced your accounts department – for example, using ResourcePhoenix (**www.resourcephoenix.com**).

For equipment purchase and other transactions, you will probably organise and authorise direct payment from your bank account. To get an online bank account, turn to page 155 of our directory – it covers the major players in the market but if you'd prefer to stick with your existing bank, they will probably have an online service – ask for details when you next visit a branch.

# 2//WORKING ONLINE

Before you can start using the Internet, you've got to get online. Whether you want to connect just one computer or the entire office network, you will need to set up an account with an Internet Service Provider (ISP), which supplies you with a route on to the net. And then you'll need to install and configure special hardware and software, connect to the net, send and receive electronic mail and browse the web. The good news is that almost all new computers now come pre-installed with all the extras you'll need, so there are just a few steps to get online. If you want comprehensive details about the basics of getting online, look at the companion title *The Virgin Guide to the Internet*.

If you've linked up not just yourself but also your colleagues at work, you'll need to consider some of the problems that come attached to the net. For example, how to deal with the threat of virus attacks, a company policy on browsing non-essential websites and avoiding any risk to office computers from hackers. In this chapter, we'll explain the pitfalls and concerns, and ensure you've got a good plan to get your business online.

## //HOW DO I CONNECT?

In theory, any computer can be connected to the Internet – from a high-powered graphics workstation to a pocket-sized personal organiser. You don't even need a computer to get the benefits of the net. If you have a mobile phone or pager, you can use this to receive information from some websites. And if your office has a network installed, you can link everyone on the network to the Internet very easily – but you will then need to install management software (see page 19).

If you're connecting just one computer, the easiest way is to use a modem and a normal phone line. If you plan to make a lot of use of the net, you'll need a faster link, such as ISDN or the new ADSL standard. In the UK, there's a small-business-friendly version of ISDN called Business Highway. But for the best compromise between speed and cost, ADSL proves hard to better. You get a permanent connection to the Internet for a fixed monthly subscription of around £50. It's many times faster than ISDN and can be a lot cheaper in call charges.

If you've an office network, it makes sense to connect the entire network to the Internet to allow all the users shared access. If there are just a couple of users or you only want email support (rather than web browsing), you can install a shared modem, but even with just a couple of users, you'll get fed up with the painfully slow download rates.

A better solution for small offices is to install a high-speed link such as an ADSL or ISDN line and share this link across the office by installing a router modem. A router bridges your office network and the outside line and automatically dials and connects to the net (within seconds) anytime someone on the network starts a web browser or email application. A specialist business ISP will be able to supply all the equipment you require, pre-configured, to connect everyone on your network to the net.

**Choosing an ISP**
An ISP is an intermediary that provides a local telephone number for your modem to dial to connect to its big computers, which form part of the Internet. Only the very biggest sites or corporations link directly to the Internet; everyone else makes use of an ISP and leaves them to manage the techie network connections.

If you plan to develop your own business website, flip to Chapter 3 to help you decide how to choose a company that can host your website. If you want to deal with just one Internet company, make sure that your future ISP can provide access and all the hosting features you require.

Essentially there are just two types of ISP: one charges and the other is free. Some countries, notably the UK, have such aggressive marketing from telephone companies and ISPs that free Internet access is common. In the latest twist to the battle, some ISPs (notably AltaVista and BT Internet) also provide free telephone calls to subscribers.

If you have colleagues within your company that travel on business and want to stay in touch, you might find an account with either AOL or CompuServe useful. Both have vast networks of telephone access numbers around the world, allowing you to stay in touch by email wherever you are.

**Office net policy**
Once you have provided everyone in the office with a link to the Internet, there's a danger that you might suddenly find productivity drops – unless you have an office policy in place and a way of policing it. There are three issues that you need to worry about:

- The threat from the outside: hackers and virus attacks.

- The problems on the inside: users accessing inappropriate sites to view smut.

- The misuse of the new channel to send libellous email messages.

The first problem has a relatively simple solution: there are plenty of security and anti-virus products available to protect a computer or network (see opposite). The second problem depends upon your company's policy. If you don't mind employees wasting hours booking their holidays online, ordering their groceries or visiting porn sites, then there's nothing to worry about. However, most companies will at least need to draw up a list of things they would rather the employees did not do. Make sure everyone knows this and respects it – and, if you want to stamp down on any infringement to these rules, you could install management software to shut down a user's session on the net as soon as they try and access a forbidden site, and send a warning message to a supervisor.

The third issue centres on one problem that's hard to crack and a nightmare to define. It concerns the way information is sent over the Internet, particularly using email; it encourages sloppy writing, gossip, or worse. Recent cases have found the company liable if employees send unwanted, libellous or harassment email messages. It's also very easy for an employee to use email for personal messages – even for job applications. It's very hard to set down even basic rules covering use of emails, let alone how they should be written. To protect themselves, many larger companies now install message-scanning utilities (see Address Book) that run on the network server and look for key words in all email messages. If a message contains words such as 'sex', 'secret' or even 'job application', the entire message can be stopped before it gets to the recipient and referred to a supervisor.

## //SECURITY

Hacker scare stories in the newspapers have ensured that most businesses treat security as a priority. In reality, the risks are low, but you should still take a range of sensible precautions to protect your company's information and make it as hard as possible for a hacker to access your company's computer's files.

### How do I avoid viruses?

Almost any file that you download from the Internet could contain a virus, but the number of incidents is very low. There are several types of virus on the loose and, although many are benign, some can delete or corrupt your computer files. Viruses are tiny, highly sophisticated programs that take advantage of a loophole in a computer system or software application. They normally burrow into another 'carrier' file – often a computer program or sometimes an email message or a Word or Excel document.

When you open or run this carrier file, the virus wakes up and does two things: first, it tries to spread to other similar files – to 'infect' them – and, second, it might try and wreak havoc on your computer. Many viruses are harmless but annoying and simply spread themselves, but the majority will try and delete files, crash your hard disk or corrupt information stored in files.

You cannot catch a virus simply by downloading a file. However, if the file you download is infected with a virus, it will be activated when you open or run the file. If you download a file or receive a file via an email attachment, it could also contain a virus, so you have to be particularly careful when dealing with attachments received from an unknown email address. Run virus scanner software before opening any email attachments.

Only a few types of file can't contain viruses: notably image files and simple web pages (however, many web pages use extra programs, called applets, to provide multimedia or special effects – and these could contain a virus).

To stop any potential problems, you should always scan newly downloaded files with a special software program that can detect and remove viruses. Two of the most popular virus detection programs are McAfee (**www.mcafee.com**) and Norton AntiVirus (**www.symantec.com**). If you have a network installed or if you use a network-based email program, make sure that the server and the workstations are protected by a virus detection program. Don't forget that eager hackers are constantly developing new viruses, so you will regularly need to download special update files to ensure your anti-virus software can catch all the latest strains.

**How do I protect against hackers?**
When you connect your computer (or your network of computers) to the Internet, you are creating a path from the Internet directly over the telephone cables to your office. If a hacker knows when you are online, they can tap into your computer with very simple

software tools; once they are in, they can read your files and delete or corrupt any other information. In practice, the chances of a hacker targeting you are slim, but it is still a threat. Oddly, the longer you spend online, the greater the chance of a hacker targeting your computer (hackers often try to link to computers in a random pattern so if you're on for hours, you might get hit). This is a particular worry if you use one of the new connection systems, such as 100, that is always 'on' (i.e. your computer is always connected to the net).

If you plan to link just one computer to the Internet, you have fewer risks and less chance of a problem – but you'll also enjoy fewer benefits than if you connect your network or all your computers to give everyone in the company access to the net. Connecting a network to the Internet can leave your company's computers open to an easy attack from a hacker. To reduce the risk, make sure that you install access control and network management software.

The best way to protect your computer system is to install what is effectively a one-way door between your computer and the Internet. You can access the Internet, but someone outside can't get to your computer via your net connection. This device is called a firewall and every company that's connected to the net should consider installing one. It acts as a filter between the Internet and your network and is your first line of defence against hackers who can otherwise access your network's computers relatively easily.

You can configure a firewall to filter out any commands that seem suspicious or malicious, or block any data that originates from a particular user or country. If you are using a router to link your network to the net then this can provide some basic firewall features, but you should ask your ISP to recommend a product that works with their system. Or ask the experience of other users in newsgroups (see page 97) – such as comp.security. Perhaps the only problem with firewalls is that they often block the special coded files called cookies, used by many shopping sites, so network users might not be able to shop online.

**How do I limit where employees surf?**
To stop employees spending hours online booking holidays, browsing porn sites, or other unsuitable material, you'll need to install a special software filter program that sits in the background acting as a big brother, checking which sites are visited.

So far, there's only one basic standard developed to help limit access to sites. PICS (Platform for Internet Content Selection) uses a voluntary rating scheme, included by the web page designer. To use this PICS information, you need either a compatible web browser (such as Internet Explorer or Netscape Navigator) or a software filter. Any of these programs will let you define the type of site that can be viewed or type of material you want to allow. Since some sites might not add this PICS rating information, or might put in the wrong type of rating, you should use ratings created by an independent third party (such as RSACi at **www.rsaci.org** or SafeSurf at **www.safesurf.com**).

Some software filters have a huge list of unsuitable, blacklisted sites and block access to these sites if the person types in the address in their web browser or tries to access a newsgroup via a newsreader. You'll need to download regular updates from the Internet so that the software's always up to date with the latest nasties. Once installed, you can configure the program and add any extra sites you particularly want to block – and even prevent access to search engines and directories that list unsuitable and obscene material.

Other software filters work by detecting keywords rather than using a block list of unwanted sites. They check what's been typed into any search engine, and also what's being displayed, to block sites that include words like 'sex'. The more advanced filters include a degree of intelligence so that they will allow users to search for or view sites about 'chicken breasts' but not 'big breasts'. The advantage of these keyword programs is that they can work seamlessly across the entire range of Internet software – including the special programs used for chat and newsgroups.

## //CONFIDENTIALITY

Electronic mail is often assumed to be secure – it's not. Anything that you send in a mail message is transferred as plain text that, in theory, any hacker (or even your own computer department) could intercept and read with little difficulty. The same applies for attachments. So before you send the secrets of your company's success by email, it's worth considering ways of keeping email messages confidential.

The simplest solution is to scramble the contents of the message using an encryption system so that only the intended recipient can read what you've written. However, most email programs (including Microsoft Outlook and Qualcomm's Eudora) give you the option to encrypt messages. The problem is that you also have to find a way to secretly send the password to the receiver. Since this is often impossible, a new encryption system was developed which side-steps the problem; known as a public-key encryption system, the most popular implementation is called PGP (Pretty Good Privacy). To use it, you need to create two keys: one public, one private – both unique to you. You can give the public key to anyone but the private one is yours alone. Anyone who wants to send you an encrypted message uses your public key to scramble the message and send you the coded data. Only you, with your private key, can unscramble the information and read the message. On the other hand, anyone who wants to decrypt a message encoded using your private key has to use your public key.

You'll need special software to generate the keys and manage the encryption process. It's all available as freeware. However, you normally need to run this software separately, convert the document you want to protect into a scrambled data file and then attach this file to an email. Alternatively, you can buy special software that integrates with your existing email program so that the whole process takes just a few clicks. Find software that will work with your email software from the official distribution site at the Massachusetts Institute of Technology (MIT) (http://web.mit.edu/network/pgp.html) or try shareware libraries such as Filez library (www.filez.com). You can also visit the PGP home site (www.pgp.com) to find commercial software.

**Digital signatures**

If you are sending a particularly important email message, you will probably want to make sure that it's not altered in any way. Similarly, if you receive an important email, you would like to know that it was sent by the person who claims to have sent it. Both problems can be solved using digital signatures that effectively freeze a message – preventing any changes en route – and prove that you, and only you, sent the message.

A digital signature is a unique sequence of numbers that proves you are who you claim to be. Like PGP, they use the technique of public-key cryptography. If you want to sign a file or document, you create two encryption keys: one public, the other private. You now use the private key to scramble your normal signature (such as your name or company details) and send this to the intended recipient. The recipient uses the public key to unscramble and verify your signature. The important element of this method is that, although many people can use the public key to verify a signer's signature, they cannot use the private key to forge digital signatures.

Working alongside digital signatures is the idea of a hash signature. This provides a way of proving that the message you sent someone has not been changed during transmission: it would be unfortunate, for example, if a contract was changed from 'do' to 'do not'. The hash signature uses complex mathematical formulae to analyse the entire text you want to protect and it then calculates a number based on the characters used. The person receiving the document runs the same program and compares hash signatures – if they are not the same, the document has been tampered with.

If used correctly, both systems are extremely secure and provide very quick and efficient ways of proving identity and protecting sensitive material from unauthorised changes. As a result, many countries are now examining the legal possibility of upholding the use of approved digital signatures within electronic documents. Currently, many US states have reworked their local laws to allow digital signatures, and US federal and other national legal bodies are working towards a totally digital future. To find out how your country's progressing, visit Digital Signature Legislation (**http://mcwis.kub.nl/~frw/people/hof/DS-lawsu.htm**). It's a tough read, but comprehensive. You may never need to sign a piece of paper again.

## //ADDRESS BOOK

### Management and filter software

*If you plan to provide shared Internet access to users on your office network, you'll need to consider installing special management and filter software. The management software lets you track what each user is doing – or sending by email – and the filters prevent users from accessing banned websites, newsgroups or chat sessions while using company equipment. Some products run on each computer and are the same programs used to protect kids from porn online. Others work on a network server and offer far more sophisticated management tools to help a business installation track its users.*

**CyberPatrol**                    **www.cyberpatrol.com**
Designed to protect kids, but it'll work just as well keeping your colleagues off the undesirable or X-rated sites.

**Cybersitter**  www.cybersitter.com
Blocks access according to a vast list of sites that contain obscene, hate or anti-social material.

**GFI Communications Ltd**  www.gficomms.com
Produces specialist management software that'll monitor the content of emails and block messages that don't fit office policy.

**NetNanny**  www.netnanny.com
Keep prying eyes of kids and businessmen from X-rated or anti-social websites and newsgroups.

**NHA**  www.nha.com
Anti-virus, security and network management software and advice supplied in equal quantities.

**Omniquad**  www.omniquad.com
Tools to monitor what users are up to on your network.

**SurfWatch**  www.surfwatch.com
Monitor and limit the areas that can be viewed from a browser.

---

**PGP**

---

*Electronic mail messages are normally sent over the net as plain text – anyone listening can read the contents (even your Internet guru or network supervisor). If you want to be sure that your email stays private and that only the intended recipient can read it, you'll need to encrypt the text: i.e. scramble the contents using a special key. One of the most popular, and safest, systems is called PGP (Pretty Good Privacy). You'll need special software that works with your email program – but it's often free. Here's where to find out more.*

**MIT distribution**  http://web.mit.edu/
**site for PGP**  network/pgp.html
The official place to find the latest copy of PGP, plus all manner of ways to tie it in with your email software.

**Network Associates**  www.nai.com
Big company secrets? This commercial developer specialises in PGP software products for the larger enterprise.

**PGP Resource Page**  http://thegate.gamers.org/~tony/pgp.html
All the information, software and legal answers you'll need to get started with PGP.

**Yahoo!'s**  www.yahoo.com/Computers_and_Internet/
**PGP Page**  Security_and_Encryption/PGP_Pretty_Good_Privacy
Yahoo's comprehensive collection of sites specialising in PGP.

---

## Digital signatures

*Pack away your fountain pen: the future lies in digital signatures. Some states and countries now allow legal documents to be signed with a digital flourish; most others are in the process of working out new legislation.*

**Digital Signature**  http://cwis.kub.nl/~frw/
**Legislation**  people/hof/DS-lawsu.htm
The latest news on the state of your country's legislation to support digital signatures.

**EFF digital**  www.eff.org/pub/
**signature archive**  Privacy/Digital_signature/
An ordered mass of information that covers just about everything to do with digital signatures.

**Legislative matrix**  www.magnet.state.ma.us/
**for digital signature**  itd/legal/matrix10.htm
State-by-state comparison on legislation for digital signatures.

**Tutorial of**  www.abanet.org/scitech/ec/isc/
**Digital signatures**  dsg-tutorial.html
Concise tutorial on how they work and why they are so important to the legal world.

## Anti-virus

*Make sure that your computer is free from malicious viruses –
install a special anti-virus program that can automatically check
any new file that's downloaded from the net or attached to an
email message. It should also be able to spot macro viruses lurking
inside a Word or Excel document. Don't forget that new viruses
are being developed all the time, so you'll need to download
update files for your anti-virus software.*

### McAfee                                    www.mcafee.com
One of the most popular anti-virus products that'll kill those viruses
before they hit your files.

### Net Paradox                               www.netparadox.com
Software to help keep your network virus free.

### NHA                                       www.nha.com
Anti-virus, security and network management software and advice
supplied in equal quantities.

### Norton AntiVirus                          www.symantec.com
Just about the best-known anti-virus program on the market. It'll
work on a single computer or on a network server, alerting you if
there's a virus and deleting it before it causes problems.

### Omniquad                                  www.omniquad.com
Tools to monitor exactly what the users on your network are up to
– and, at the same time, protect them from virus attacks.

# 3//YOUR OWN WEBSITE

Don't just use the Internet as a library – instead, join in. Create a website for your company and market your brand and products to a vast new audience of potential customers. Here are a few of the reasons why companies have set up their own sites:

- to increase their customer base across the world

- to provide a permanent display of all their products, with reviews, explanations and links to local distributors

- to sell products directly from their website

- to advertise a new range or product – or simply to promote their brand

- to provide all the background information a customer might require, so cutting down the number of catalogues they send out

- to provide support and answers to common questions about the product range, cutting down on support phone calls

- to provide a forum for customers, reps and journalists to get the latest information about the company.

When you're planning your new website, make sure that it's not just a boring catalogue of products. You want to try to provide content that will attract visitors, then ensure that there's enough of a community feel to keep them on your site and, finally, integrate an e-commerce section to pay for the costs of providing the content. These three key factors are often called the three Cs: Content, Community and Commerce. Make sure that your site addresses them all.

In the old days, you would need a degree in programming and a helpful ISP to get even a modest business website up and running.

Now, it's easy to create a site – although a well-designed business site will take considerable planning to get right.

To start with, consider why you are creating your site. If you want to raise brand awareness, you'll need to promote the brand, logo and colours together with a simple message that's relevant across the site. And since you're promoting the brand rather than a service or product, you'll need to offer plenty of useful information and resources to get people to visit. If, however, your site concentrates on selling products, you'll need to provide a design that loads quickly and offers a fast, efficient route to help customers find and pay for a product.

This chapter includes ideas on how to build the content of your site and make it 'sticky' – so that visitors won't want to leave. Make sure that your site is useful, interesting, user-friendly and up to date. Don't just create an online version of your catalogue – that's too dull. You might get an initial surge of visitors, but the numbers will soon tail off. Better to create a site that's interesting and informative where the number of visitors keeps increasing.

## //FINANCING A WEBSITE

Creating a sophisticated website is not cheap. Yes, you can create a fantastic site for next to nothing, but only if you're an experienced designer, programmer, writer and editor with lots of spare time. Since you're probably busy running a business, you'll need to ask experts to help with each stage. And this is where the costs start to escalate.

A basic website that you create yourself can cost as little as £10 ($15) per month – to rent the web space. A designer will probably cost a few thousand pounds (or dollars), depending upon the complexity of your site, and you will probably need a programmer or specialist to create interactive features such as a database, response form or multimedia effects. E-commerce sites can easily double the costs, with potentially high initial costs for shopping cart software, web space and items such as security certificates. To provide a rich user environment, you'll need to hire a writer to create content, or pay to license content (for example, words, pictures, news, weather or share prices) from another company. And to ensure that everyone works together, you should use a specialist web management company to oversee the project.

A modest website can easily cost £30,000 ($50,000) to set up; a complex e-commerce site to rival giants such as Amazon, could cost up to a million, or more. And then there are day-to-day running costs for staff and support, legal fees to ensure copyright and content protection, distribution and fulfilment costs (if you're selling something) and bank charges.

Unless your company has deep pockets and is willing to invest in this new technology, you'll probably need to raise finance to pay for the site's development and running costs till it has started to generate an income. You could try your bank for a loan or overdraft or use one of the specialist banks listed on page 161 that arrange venture capital or high-tech loans for just such a project. Before you approach either your bank or a specialist, make sure that you have prepared your sales material carefully. Create a business plan (see page 126 for details of sites that can help), spend time online to see what works and what doesn't and come up with key points that differentiate your site and its content from the others already online.

## //YOUR OWN WEBSITE ADDRESS

Sign up with any ISP and you'll get an allocation of web space that has its own unique address, normally called its URL (Uniform Resource Locator), that lets any other user find and view your site. When you get an account with the Internet provider, it will tell you your URL: it's normally made up of the provider's name and your user name. For example, if you sign up with Virgin Net and your user name is OKPlumbing, your website would be at www.virgin.net/OKPlumbing. If you were with Demon Internet, the address would be www.okplumbing.demon.co.uk.

If you want to be taken seriously on the web, it's almost essential to establish your presence by registering your own unique name – called a domain name. It doesn't do much for your image if you promote an email address at AOL or a website hosted on a free ISP such as Freeserve. It's also worth registering your domain name before someone else gets the same idea, and so protect your brand name.

Carrying on with our example, www.okplumbing.co.uk might be a good home. The simplest way to register your own domain name is to ask your Internet provider to do the work for you. You'll have to pay an initial registration fee and then a yearly subscription just to maintain your own domain name (it's normally between £40 and £100 ($60-$150) per year). If you want to register the name yourself, visit one of the main registration services such as **www.netbenefit.co.uk** or view a list of registrars at InterNIC (**www.internic.net**). And, to date, you cannot yet have your own domain name with any of the free web space providers, nor with AOL or CompuServe.

**What's acceptable?**
Anything goes on the Internet, but that's not necessarily true of the company that's providing the disk space to store your website. All web space providers have their own Acceptable User Policy (AUP) that spells out exactly what you can and cannot do with your account. Many won't let you sell products or run commercial sites from a free account. Others don't want offensive material. If you break the AUP, your account will be closed down and you'll have to find another provider.

## //HOW DO I BUILD IT?

A website is a collection of individual pages that contain different elements: descriptive text, graphic images and perhaps an advanced feature such as a response form or database link. Your company probably already has a logo and perhaps a corporate colour scheme – don't forget to reflect this in the website design. If you used a designer for your catalogue or publicity material then it's tempting to use the same person to create your site. But print and web are very different media, so make sure you choose a designer who has experience of the requirements – and limitations – of the web. Alternatively you can do the job yourself, using the templates supplied with most web design software and a little imagination.

Designing the page is rather like using a sophisticated word processor: you can type in text, add headlines, change the fonts and add in images and animation – even video clips. All these different elements of a web page are described using a special set of codes called HTML (HyperText Markup Language) – so you need to use a program that enables you to create pages using HTML commands.

---

Don't go overboard with fonts, colours and images. Look at lots of other sites to see what works for you. Take a look at Yahoo! (www.yahoo.com) for the clean design look, CD Now (www.cdnow.com) as an example of an efficient e-commerce site, or Web Pages That Suck (www.webpagesthatsuck.com) for examples of truly dreadful designs.

---

The most flexible and powerful way to create a web page is to use a special web page design program such as Microsoft FrontPage, NetObjects Fusion or Adobe Dreamweaver – but these can take a while to learn. If you want to experiment, you can get started using an up-to-date word-processing application such as Word or WordPerfect – or one of the free simple page design programs supplied with both Microsoft's Internet Explorer and Netscape's Navigator web browsers. However, these methods are really just for fun. You'll find it impossible to create and manage a large business site with a word processor.

Once you've decided to create the killer business site, the sensible solution is to use one of the specialised web page editing programs (often called web authoring software) that give you complete control over all the parts of a web page. Most authoring software is sold as a commercial product, but you can download trial versions that will run for 30 days before you have to pay. Visit Builder (www.builder.com), WebMonkey (www.webmonkey.com) or Filez (www.filez.com) to download a time-limited demo of some of the main programs.

The best-known web authoring programs include Microsoft FrontPage (www.microsoft.com/frontpage), Adobe Dreamweaver (www.adobe.com), and NetObjects Fusion (www.netobjects.com). All three provide different tools and features and allow the user to create and manage a large collection of web pages.

### Adding pictures

There's a balancing act when creating images for the web between image quality, image size and the time it will take to display the picture. You want to try to create high-quality, colourful images that are stored in a file that's as small as possible – so they are quick to download and display. Include too many images, or use files that are too big, and users will give up on your site. Most visitors don't like waiting more than 20 seconds for a page to display, so try to limit yourself to just two or three images for each page.

---

Try to keep the size of all the files used on any page below 40Kb – that includes images, main page and sound. Any bigger and it will take too long to display and the visitor will get bored.

---

The size of an image file is determined by the number of colours used, the size of the image and the resolution. Image editing programs – such as the popular shareware Paintshop Pro (**www.jasc.com**) – let you adjust all three till you reach the perfect balance between quality and file size.

Avoid over-design when creating your website. If you have lots of images in a printed catalogue, it looks great. However, if you have lots of images on a web page, it simply takes longer to display – impatient potential customers will give up waiting for all the images to download and go elsewhere.

### Adding links

The web was designed to allow you link one page to another, or one site to another, so that a user can follow the links and travel around the web. Your mouse pointer changes to a pointing hand when it passes over a link. Almost any element on a web page can be turned into a link: text, an image, or even just a small part of an image.

If you have divided up the information you want to publish into separate web pages, you'll need to add links between each page so that visitors can navigate through the site and jump from one page to the next.

---

When you build your site, think what you would like if you were a visitor. Include plenty of resources such as links to other sites that a visitor will find useful – it helps builds the sense of a community!

---

### Using a web design company

You can create a stunning, sophisticated, feature-packed website on the cheap – if you're prepared to do all the work yourself. However, most companies have neither the time nor the programming and design expertise to plan and implement a basic site, let alone something as complicated as an interactive e-commerce online shop. If you want to put up a simple catalogue site with pictures of your products and services, you can buy a web page design package and create a basic but effective presence on the web. It'll cost you the price of the software and a monthly rental fee for web space where you can publish your site (see above).

Most businesses, however, will prefer to turn to a specialist web design company that they can work with to plan the structure and design of their site. And if you want to set up an online shop that can accept credit card payments, you'll find a specialist saves time and money in organising a merchant account and certificate of authentication (see page 47), installing the software and helping load the shopping cart software with details of all your products.

Web design companies normally work on a per-project fee basis; once you have both agreed on the content of the site, you'll get an estimate of the time and costs required. One of the biggest problems is trying to find a web design company that you think will do a good job on your site. Specialist web-business magazine sites normally include directories of design companies; try Internet Works (www.iwks.com) or Business 2.0 (www.business2.com). Next time you are browsing on the net, make a note of the sites you think are well designed and effective in promoting their message – you'll normally find a credit to the design company that developed the site somewhere on the home page.

**Content and community**

To provide a sticky website (one that visitors don't want to leave), business sites are usually packed with content and advanced features. Many have features such as a discussion group, or allow visitors to search a database, buy products or send in comments. These features are normally created using a special program that works through a system called CGI (which provides the path from a web page to the program that runs on the server).

To add any of these features to your site, you'll probably need to install special software – either ask your web space provider, buy a commercial product or use a free Perl script from ScriptSearch (**www.scriptsearch.com**). Here are some of the most popular ways you can add content and a feeling of community to your website:

- Discussion groups add activity with little effort on your part (see Chapter 8 for more on using discussion groups). Visitors can chat between themselves or ask you for advice or support.

- Set up a mailing list (often called a listserver) and encourage visitors to subscribe by typing in their email address; you can use the mailing list both to distribute information to the subscribers and to provide a forum in which the subscribers can exchange ideas.

- Make sure that there are pages on your website that include feedback forms to help users request further information, send comments or complaints, or ask for technical support.

- A guest book is a simple way of encouraging visitors to leave their comments about your site or products that can then be read by any other visitor.

- Include a page of links to related online resources that your customers might find useful. For example, a builder might have links to the various professional building trade organisations, specialist suppliers of bricks, enthusiast sites about heritage paint styles, preservation societies, handmade kitchen units or even antiques – anything related to home improvement.

- Provide pages with support and tips-and-tricks to help your customers get the most from your products.

- Databases are very popular – if they contain something useful! If you are a pharmacist, you might have a database of the names of medicines or even an online dictionary or glossary.

- Maps are useful. Most of the major hotels include interactive maps, often supplied by specialist companies such as MapQuest (**www.mapquest.com**), that let visitors see exactly where the hotel is located in a city.

## Advanced features

Most of the advanced applications that you see on websites, such as shopping carts, quizzes, or database links, have been created using a programming language called Perl. If you have the time, you could learn Perl and write your own programs – it's not the most complicated language, but it is still a challenge for non-programmers. Visit the Perl archives (**www.perl.org**) for information and help.

Alternatively, visit one of the vast libraries of free and shareware programs written in Perl by other programmers. SuperScripts (**www.superscripts.com**) and ScriptSearch (**www.scriptsearch.com**) have hundreds of complete application programs to enhance your website. It sounds very easy, but it can take several days to get a Perl program working properly on your site.

The alternative to the DIY approach of Perl is to buy a commercial product that is ready to install and run. It can be hard to justify the (often high) cost of commercial web software but, unless you're prepared to spend days or weeks tinkering under the bonnet of a Perl program, it's often money well spent. One last hurdle is that any program, such as a shopping cart application, normally has to be installed on the server computer where your website is stored. Almost all web space providers let you run Perl programs (often called scripts) but they might charge extra to install and run a commercial product.

### Adding a database to your site

One of the most popular 'advanced' features added to a website is to allow visitors to search a database. If you've looked for a book on Amazon (www.amazon.com), tried to find a CD on CD Now (www.cdnow.com) or searched for a new printer at Action Computers (www.action.com), you've been using a database. More obvious database applications include Yellow Pages (www.bigyellow.com), directories of business sites, such as the Biz (www.thebiz.co.uk) and telephone directories to help you find staff within a vast company, such as IBM (www.ibm.com).

If you want to add a database to your website, you could use a free Perl script from ScriptSearch and install this on your website's server computer. Alternatively, you could use a specialist web page design program such as Microsoft FrontPage, which has database support built in to let you add an Access database to your website (but needs special FrontPage features configured by your web space provider). Or you could use a stand-alone commercial database product such as FileMaker Pro (www.filemaker.com) – which again requires support from your web space provider. If you plan on adding any of these advanced features, you'll find it useful to talk to your hosting company; they probably don't support some of the technologies but they might have a different solution available.

### Java, JavaScript and cookies

The basic foundation of any web page is created using HTML commands, but there are several different ways of adding to the rather limited features of HTML. Java and JavaScript are among the best known, and they let you add all kinds of 'bells and whistles' to your web page. Java is a sophisticated programming language that's used to create small programs (called applets) that can be run by a browser. For example, some shopping carts, financial calculators and multimedia special effects are created using Java applets. JavaScript is a kind of extension to HTML that lets you add natty effects to your web page, such as displaying a pop-up window, changing the colour of text as the mouse moves over it, creating simple animation or playing music when the page is displayed. The JavaScript commands are written within the web page file so that when a browser loads a web page, it will follow both the HTML and JavaScript commands.

Unless you plan to dedicate your life to programming, forget Java. Instead, visit JavaScript sites that are packed with information about the language: try JavaScript (www.javascript.com), WebMonkey (www.webmonkey.com) or Builder (www.builder.com). All three include example snippets of JavaScript code that you can cut and paste into your web pages to add life to a tired design.

Many business and e-commerce sites keep track of regular visitors using a feature called a 'cookie'. Cookies are scraps of information stored in a file on the user's computer; any site can create its own marker in this file using simple JavaScript (or Perl) commands. The marker could include the user's registered name, when they last visited the site or the last item they ordered from a shop. Once customers have registered on your site, you can greet them by name next time they visit – thanks to cookies.

---

### Different browsers

Not all users have the same web browser software installed – which can be terribly frustrating for a web page designer who wants to make the most of the latest features. Some new design tricks only work on Microsoft IE, others only on Netscape Navigator.

If you use advanced web design features or snazzy JavaScript commands, you'll end up with a site that can only be properly appreciated on just one of the two types of browser. If you want to cater for the widest audience, don't use the newest tricks. If you do, you'll alienate half your visitors. And if you plan on creating a site that'll appeal to every possible user, don't forget to provide a plain text site for users connecting via mobile phones and PDAs.

Visit BrowserWatch (**www.browserwatch.com**) to find out the current state of the battle between the browsers. A common solution is to create two similar sites; one with cool features, one without. A tiny program (either in JavaScript or Perl) automatically detects the type of browser a visitor is using and redirects them to a correct part of the site.

## //GETTING WEB SPACE

If you keep the collection of pages that have been designed for your company's new website on your desktop computer, you'll be the only one who can enjoy their depth and vision. Publish them – 'upload' them – to a public Internet server and the rest of the Internet world will be able to view your company's products.

Your ISP will provide you with a certain amount of free web space that you can use to store your website. Both free and charging ISPs will supply you with web space as part of your account. If you are using a free ISP (such as Freeserve or Virgin Net) then you pay nothing, but you cannot have your own domain name, drive a complex database or fix up a live video address from the chairman.

In contrast, paid ISPs also provide web space but do, generally, offer extra features for business users. Most of the larger ISPs are re-orientating themselves to provide a complete range of services for business sites, from design to e-commerce.

One of the most popular routes is to sign up with a company that only offers web space. These companies, sometimes called virtual servers, won't provide access numbers for you to browse the Internet – simply a place where you can store your site. They offer masses of features at a low price – because they don't have to spend their money on expensive telephone equipment to provide users with access to the net. If you choose a hosting provider, you'll still need to sign up with an ISP to use the Internet.

### Publishing a website

To allow public access to your website, you have to copy all the individual files (that make up each page, together with any images, program scripts and database files) to the web space on your provider's server computer. Once the files are on the provider's server, anyone on the Internet will be able to view the site.

To copy a file over the Internet, you use a system called FTP (file transfer protocol). FTP is just a set of simple commands, but you'll need a special FTP program that works rather like the Windows Explorer – there are dozens freely available from sites such as Filez (www.filez.com). You need to configure the FTP program with the user name, password and the address of the area of web space on the server; the company that's hosting your site provides all three when you sign up.

If you are using any of the mainstream web page design programs (such as FrontPage, NetObjects or Dreamweaver), you'll avoid direct contact with FTP: these page design programs have a menu option that will automatically publish all your files to the provider's server.

## //ADDRESS BOOK

---

#### Advice for site builders

---

*Web tools and programming systems keep changing and evolving, so the best places to find out the latest are the sites dedicated to web developers.*

**Builder.com**                                          **www.builder.com**
Visit this vast site for great features, reviews and discussion on topics ranging from basic design to cutting-edge programming.

**Pages That Suck**                    **www.pagesthatsuck.com**
Two top designers tell you what not to do.

**WebDeveloper**                       **www.webdeveloper.com**
Every web developer's home from home, with news, features and how-tos.

**WebMonkey**                          **www.webmonkey.com**
Comprehensive, advanced but accessible guides to building your own site; full of tips, tricks and reviews of gizmos to make your web development easier.

---

### Web page editors

*You can try out your web coding techniques with any word processor or the tools supplied with web browsers. However, any serious website needs more sophisticated design features and ways of managing the files and links. This range of programs will provide all you need to design and manage the most complex of sites.*

**Dreamweaver**                        **www.adobe.com**
Swish design program that lets you create great-looking sites packed with multimedia and effects.

**Fusion**                             **www.netobjects.com**
Lets non-programmers concentrate on building large, complex design-friendly sites.

**FrontPage**                          **www.microsoft.com**
Microsoft's site design software – has stacks of clever tricks, but needs a host that supports it.

**HotDog**                             **www.sausage.com**
Cool and trendy function-rich page design software, but best for techies.

### HoTMetaL
www.sq.com

Back-to-basics page design and editing software for programmers who take life seriously.

### LinkBot
www.linkbot.com

Scans your website for broken links – before your visitors find them. Most good website design tools should have this feature built in.

### PageMill
www.adobe.com

Manage your site and design your page using this visual, DTP-style program.

### Visual Page
www.symantec.com

General-purpose site design, with good Java support (for Symantec's range of Java development software).

---

### Adding a database

*Adding a database – often of product information and prices – to a website is one of the main features of many business sites. But you'll need to talk to your website host to see if they support common software solutions – such as FrontPage or FileMaker – and if not, you might have to use a primitive, but flexible, program written in Perl from a library such as ScriptSearch.*

### Borland
www.borland.com

Range of high-end, complex database products that'll power your site, but will also require a programmer.

### FileMaker Pro
www.filemaker.com

Popular, relatively easy way of designing a web-friendly database – if your hosting company supports it.

### Microsoft
www.microsoft.com

A few clicks and you can link an Access database to your FrontPage site – if your hosting company allows.

**Microrim**  www.microrim.com
Mighty big database? High-power software to manage it.

**Oracle**  www.oracle.com
Oracle software drives thousands of leading websites – it's expensive, and it needs expertise and resources, but provides impressive performance and features.

**ScriptSearch**  www.scriptsearch.com
Vast collection of free and shareware Perl, Java and C programs that offer database access – but you should brush up your programming first.

---

**Programming resources**

*Anything other than a basic page layout will need some form of extra programming. Perl ranks as the most popular programming language on the web – with stacks of free example programs.*

**ActiveX**  www.microsoft.com
Microsoft's answer to Java – allows serious developers to extend website functionality.

**BrowserWatch**  www.browserwatch.com
If you're programming like crazy, keep up to date with the latest news on web browser features that you can exploit.

**Clipart.com**  www.clipart.com
Great directory of the main clip art sites around the web, each with thousands of icons, pictures, animated gizmos and buttons to copy and use on your site.

**Freescripts**  www.freescripts.com
Add an auction or shopping cart to your site. Hundreds of free and shareware Perl and JavaScript scripts.

**Java**  www.java.com
Develop your own programs to push your browser to the limit.

**JavaScript**                               **www.javascript.com**

Enhance your website with cool effects using this library of
JavaScript routines.

**Perl programming language**                **www.perl.org**

What is this Perl thingy, why is it so important and how come it's so
widely used on the web?

**ScriptSearch**                             **www.scriptsearch.com**

About the best (and biggest) collection of free and shareware Perl,
JavaScript and C programs to enhance your website.

**Shockwave**                                **www.macromedia.com**

Like those cool multimedia tricks? They were probably created with
Shockwave.

# 4//E-COMMERCE

Trading on the Internet gives you a new outlet that's open all hours. It's a shop dedicated to your products, it's cheap to run and low on overheads. You'll attract a new customer base, and you can improve relations with the existing customers. It's fast to set up, has low start-up costs compared to a high-street shop and staffing is minimal. As a result, the arrival of e-commerce has transformed many traditional businesses.

You can use e-commerce to help your existing company reach a new range of customers or you can start a totally new company servicing a particular niche market. Because the costs are low, you can compete on an even footing with your biggest competitors and, on occasion, even win. However, it is one of the most complex parts of any website to set up.

Here are some of the benefits of an online shop:

- It's a new outlet that's dedicated to your products.
- Some international customers might even find it more convenient to shop online than via your normal distributor.
- Once set up, an online shop is very efficient – with low running costs and few employee costs.
- You can manage cashflow by purchasing stock on a just-in-time basis.
- You can widen your customer base and improve service to existing customers.
- You can improve marketing knowledge of your customers: test special offers easily and link products directly to advertisements.
- Customers without a local distributor can order your goods directly.

- You can track each customer's buying habits to make it easier for customers to reorder favourite goods.

In this chapter, we'll explain what you need, where to find it and how it all works.

**What sells?**

One of the best-known names online is the Amazon bookshop (www.amazon.com). It defined the way to sell books cheaply and effectively to customers. Amazon also ensured that the buying process was as simple as possible and the site directly involves the visitors – by allowing them to write reviews of books.

Amazon was the first site to demonstrate that the simplest products to sell are those that appeal to the net's core audience of young men – this means games, software, books, CDs and the like. But the user profile of the net is changing fast and you'll find a good cross-section of all ages, men and women, shopping for stuff they can't find on the high street.

Niche products, especially local or specialist goods, sell very well. For example, there are hundreds of shops selling local foods – including salmon from Scotland, whiskey from Ireland, pastrami from New York, pasta from Italy and coffee from Seattle.

Look at *The Virgin Internet Shopping Guide* for a vast range of shops that sell everything from fridges to carpets, cars to wine. Even Amazon has diversified and has now re-invented itself as a general online shop. So, whether you manufacture copper pipes or sewing kits, grow plants or work as an interior designer, you'll find that the online community is now ready to buy just about anything.

## //HOW TO GET STARTED

To start up your shop on the Internet, you'll need two specialist products. First, you'll need special shopping cart software that mimics a real shop and shopping process: it displays the range of products and lets a visitor browse and put products into their virtual shopping basket. Second, you need a mechanism to accept and confirm credit card payments from the shopper.

---

Not all shops need shopping carts. If you sell information, advice or software then you simply ask for payment, then allow the user to download the data once you've been paid.

---

### Shopping cart software

If you browse or buy anything from an online shop, you're actually using a specialist shopping cart software program. This complex software manages a database of often thousands of products, individually tracks each customer to the site, displays the product information and manages the shopping – and paying – process.

---

#### The shopping cart in action

Here's the typical shopping process. A customer enters a shop, browses and chooses an item, which is then added to their personal virtual shopping basket. Once the customer's finished browsing, they can move to the checkout area, where the shopping cart software calculates the total cost and adds any tax and shipping. To pay for the products, the customer types in their credit card number (although there are other methods); this is sent for authorisation by a bank, and a receipt is sent by email to the customer. Soon afterwards, the products bought are delivered – either via the post or, sometimes, electronically.

---

Choose the wrong cart software and you'll consign yourself and your customers to an unnecessarily painful shopping experience. There are dozens of different shopping cart products available: some are free, some flexible, some require a programmer to install and some can support thousands of product lines. They fall into two main categories. One is an online template solution that lets you set up your own shop by answering a series of questions on a specialist website; follow the procedure and it will create a functional online shop that is ready to accept customers. Alternatively, you can buy a customised software program that has been developed or configured for your company and its products, but this will need to be installed on your website (a process that often requires the help of a programmer).

**Turnkey shopping carts** These products are great for new, small shops or people who don't want to spend a fortune in time and money creating a custom shop. These products are available for a monthly rental from specialist business Internet companies such as Virgin's own VirginBiz (**www.virginbiz.net**), Yahoo! Store (**http://store.yahoo.com**), Demon Commerce (**www.demon.net**) and iCat (**www.icat.com**).

The software is very easy to use: you'll get design templates for a shop and a near-automatic web-based system of creating your shop. All the complex program set-up is automated and hidden. You pay a monthly rental, normally between £30 and £200 ($50-300) depending upon the number of products you want to sell in the shop. If you already have a website, you can link the shop to your main site. If you don't, this is a good way to kill two birds with one stone.

Some of the biggest players in this market are the vast portals, such as Yahoo! Store (**http://store.yahoo.com**), Amazon zShops (**www.amazon.com/zshops/**) and Excite! Shopping (**http://shopping.excite.com**). One distinct advantage of these sites is that you get added exposure within their search index – making it easier for visitors to find you.

**Custom shopping carts** If you have the expertise and inclination, you can install a custom shopping cart software program for a fraction of the cost of running a turnkey product. Some shopping cart software is free – try one of the software libraries such as ScriptSearch (www.scriptsearch.com) – while others, such as Cows (www.cows.co.uk) and ShopAssistant (www.actinic.co.uk), are sold commercially. Prices for these depend on how many sophisticated features are built into the software; for example, some advanced shopping cart programs support loyalty discount schemes for frequent shoppers.

Installing and configuring a custom shopping cart program is rarely easy: you'll often need expert help to configure the software and install it into your website. However, once this is done, you'll normally have a far more flexible and powerful shopping product than one created via a template-driven solution. If you are planning a large shop, with hundreds of products, or if you want to provide complex discounts, affiliate schemes or any of the other gimmicks of online shopping, you'll probably find these features are only available by using a custom shopping cart program.

Installing new shopping cart software must rate as one of the most irritating, and often needlessly complicated, jobs that you'll have to do. If your online shop is big or complex, you would be well advised to hire a specialist web development company that can manage the project for you. If you have a smaller shop, it can be tempting to do the work yourself. Installing free or shareware products is very difficult and requires a good knowledge of the Perl programming language. Some commercial products, such as Actinic (www.actinic.com), include a special configuration program that runs on your desktop computer. This allows you to design and create your shop, before installing the entire software on your website automatically.

### Shopping malls
Instead of bothering with the fuss of choosing, installing and designing a new shop with shopping cart software, you could set up within a community of shops – normally called a shopping mall.

The advantage is that there's more on offer to tempt in visitors, it's easy for customers to browse the different shops and the technology is already developed and proven – and it's easy to install. One of the best known is pioneer BarclaySquare (www.barclaysquare.co.uk), but there are others such as eDirectory (www.edirectory.co.uk). Some malls provide a complete service, including payment processing, for a monthly fee. Others provide all the services free, in exchange for an often very high percentage charge of any sale you make.

---

**Keep it private**

Most consumers want to protect their privacy on the Internet. If your website asks a customer to type in their personal details, address or credit card details, you are in a position of trust. You could misuse this information – send them unwanted advertisements or, worse, sell the material on to a mailing list company. Most reputable online shops now have a privacy code. To gain the respect of your customers, make sure that your shop has one – outlining what you do with any information and what you promise not to do. The best advice is to store all your customer information securely on your computers and never to resell the data to any other company.

---

## //ACCEPTING PAYMENT

The most commonly accepted currency for payment on the Internet is the credit card: it's convenient, flexible, relatively safe and most shoppers have one. It's easy enough to create a simple web page that allows a customer to type in their name, address and credit card details, but what happens next?

There are two ways of completing the shopping process. First, the usual and favoured route is to automatically check and authorise the customer's credit card – within a couple of seconds you can confirm to the customer that their order has been accepted. The second alternative is to process the credit card manually as you pack the order ready to send off. This is cheaper and less complex to set up, but it gets in the way of a hands-off automatic shopping process.

## Authorising credit cards

Almost all online shops choose to use a real-time authorisation process. Processing a customer's credit card should be simple and fast – or the customer will get bored and go somewhere else. To authorise a card, you'll need to use a specialist company that will take information from the shopping cart software and carry out the process automatically. Once the credit card has been authorised, the total cost is debited from the customer's card account and transferred to your bank account.

---

Each country has its own range of card processing companies, but the majority are based in the United States. Some of these are happy to do business with non-US companies, others will only work with you if you have a US merchant account.

---

To authorise credit card payments, you'll need to set up an account with the specialist card processing company, such as WorldPay (www.worldpay.com), SecureTrading (www.securetrading.com) or NetBanx (www.netbanx.com). Make sure that the processing company's computer systems and software can be easily linked to your shopping cart software. If not, you'll need either to hire a programmer to fix the interface or to choose a different product.

## Internet merchant accounts

In order to work with a company that can authorise and process credit cards, you'll need an Internet credit card merchant account with one of the major clearing banks. (If you want to accept American Express, you'll need to set up a separate account directly with AmEx.) If your company already accepts credit cards, you'll need another, different Internet merchant account to accept payment via the Internet. Start this application process as early as possible: it normally takes from four to six weeks to get a new Internet merchant account.

The alternative is to use a bureau – most of the authorisation companies offer this service. You'll be charged a higher fee, but you won't need a new merchant account; instead, you use the bureau's merchant account. It's a quick and convenient solution for companies that want to test the market without the hassle and expense of setting up new accounts.

### Costs

There are four different costs to take into account when setting up your Internet shop:

- the set-up costs
- the running costs in maintaining your site and shop and ensuring that they're up to date
- the processing costs in accepting payments, and
- the distribution costs in fulfilling the customer's order.

Some of these costs are paid as a fee, sometimes in advance, while others are paid as a percentage of total sales when the sale is completed. A virtual shop might cut down on the costs of staff and premises, but make sure that all these new costs are covered in your business model.

**Set-up costs** Creating a new shop will incur set-up costs. These will normally include purchasing any special software – such as the shopping cart program – and paying your Internet hosting company provider for security features such as SSL (see below). And, if you have a complex project, you might have to hire a designer and programmer to manage the creation and installation of your shop.

**Running costs** Compared to the rents on the high street, even the biggest virtual shop costs very little to run. You will need to pay a monthly rental to your Internet hosting provider for web space and any extra security features you have requested (usually £30-100/$50-150). If you have chosen to use a turnkey shopping cart, you will probably have to pay a monthly rental (usually £40-200/$60-300). And the company that carries out credit card authorisation might request a yearly service charge (normally around £100/$150). Don't forget that you will also need to allocate running costs to hiring specialist staff who can manage the site, keep the information up to date, answer customer queries and complaints and also package and send out any orders.

**Processing costs** Whenever someone makes a purchase at your shop, you will incur a variety of processing costs. The company that provides the credit card authorisation service will usually charge a percentage fee (normally 1-4%) for each transaction. The bank that manages your Internet merchant account will also require a percentage fee (1-4%).for each transaction.

**Distribution costs** If a distributor or specialist warehouse carries out your order fulfilment and distribution functions, you can expect to pay 6-15% for their work in picking the items, packing and sending off the order.

## //A SAFE SHOPPING ENVIRONMENT

Consumers are, after a couple of years of uncertainty, beginning to trust the security measures that are part of secure, well-designed online shops. The problem is that, because of its fundamental design, the Internet is not a secure system – it's relatively easy for a hacker to 'listen' into to your online session and see exactly what's on your screen. To get around this, if you plan to ask a customer to type in personal details or a credit card number, you'll need to provide a secure link that scrambles all the data flowing between their computer and your website.

The main security system used in e-commerce is called SSL (Secure Sockets Layer). Its great advantage is that it does not involve any extra work or effort from the user. If you want to install SSL on your website to protect customer information, you'll need to ask your website hosting company to add this feature.

The key to SSL is a unique number, called the certificate of authentication, which is issued to every person who installs SSL. These certificates are issued by a few trusted companies: on receipt of sufficient proof that your company is genuine and sound, you'll get a certificate that can then be used to create your SSL secure area and shown to any user who wants proof that your website is run by you. The trusted company issuing the certificate will charge you a set-up fee and a renewal fee each year – around £150/$200 each. Any good hosting company will be able to help you apply for a certificate and set up a secure area of your website where you can store the pages that request personal data from users.

If the thought of filling in more forms and sending off company registration documents to the certificate issuer sounds like too much bother, there is an alternative. Most hosting companies will offer either to 'lend' you their certificate or to help you apply for your own certificate under your company's name. Both of these solutions are equally secure, but if you want to reassure your customers, you should ask your hosting company to apply for an authentication licence on your behalf. However, in practice most customers aren't too worried about who has the certificate, so long as the site is secure.

**How secure sites work**
When customers click to enter the secure area of a website, the site's web server sends their browser program a signal to switch to secure mode. When the browser replies, the server sends over its certificate of authentication (this is a unique series of numbers), which is then checked with the specialist company that issued the certificate (such as VeriSign or Thawte) to make sure that the

certificate belongs to the company that's using it. If the company is sharing the certificate with their Internet provider, it's still a safe channel, but not quite as reassuring as the company having their own certificate. For the full details, customers can double click on the padlock or key icon in the status bar of your browser – it'll tell them who issued the certificate and the company it belongs to.

Once the certificate has been sent over by the company, it is used by both browser and server to create a special code that will scramble data as it is sent from one to the other. The encryption technology is based on military coding methods, so it is very powerful. Anything customers type in on the web page is encrypted before being sent over the Internet, and it has to be unscrambled by the keyholder at the other end. Similarly, only the customers' browser can unscramble any data sent to them. Determined hackers could still intercept the information as it moves across the network, but they would never be able to unscramble it.

When the server and the browser have established the secure channel, a tiny closed padlock icon is displayed in the status bar at the bottom of the browser window. All current versions of web browsers, including Microsoft Internet Explorer and Netscape Navigator, support SSL.

Another, older system that is sometimes still used to provide a secure website is called S-HTTP. It provides a way of sending messages securely over the net to form an effective secure website (whereas SSL provides a channel over which any message can be transferred). The problem with S-HTTP is that it's not very well supported by web browsers – but they all support the prevalent SSL standard.

---

**Low-cost security**
If you want to provide a way for customers to send sensitive, personal or payment details to your company but don't want to set up SSL or a credit card payment scheme,

you could provide a secure email link. It's simple and effective and was common in the early days of e-commerce, but now it's rare and mainly used as a way of communicating with existing customers.

The standard way of implementing a secure email link is to use PGP (see page 17). You'll find all the free software and instructions online – try the official distribution site at the Massachusetts Institute of Technology (MIT) (**http://web.mit.edu/network/pgp.html**) or shareware libraries such as Filez library (**www.filez.com**). You can also visit the PGP home site (**www.pgp.com**) to find commercial software.

### Digital money.
For the moment, credit cards are still the predominant and most important method of payment on the Internet. If you set up a shop online, you'll need to accept credit card payments – or your customers will go elsewhere. But credit cards have their problems, and there are new payment methods that you need to be aware of – once consumers start to use a different system, you'll need to change your shop. To keep up to date with the latest news on what's happening in online payment, visit CommerceNet (**www.commerce.com**).

The main problem with credit cards is that the high processing charges mean that they only work efficiently when you're spending a reasonable amount – they are no good as a replacement for petty cash. For example, a credit card is a great way to buy books, CDs, computers or clothes over the net, but if you want to read a journal or watch a video online, which will only cost a few pounds or dollars, the processing costs will seem disproportionately high. To get around this, banks (and the credit-card companies themselves) are developing ways to provide a convenient electronic replacement for cash.

The future will probably consist of a smart card loaded up with electronic credit and a web browser that manages this 'electronic wallet' for you when you buy and sell online. This is ideal if you're asked for a few pence or cents to read a book, check a newsletter or watch a video. In fact, this model has already arrived, but there are still very few shops or customers taking advantage of it. To find out the latest, visit the developers of this technology such as Mondex (**www.mondex.com**), DigiCash (**www.digicash.com**), VisaCash (**www.visa.com**) and Barclaycoin (**www. barclaycoin.co.uk**).

---

### SET: the next big thing?

A new payment and security system, Secure Electronic Transmission (SET), has been developed by leading computer and credit card companies (including Microsoft, IBM, Visa and MasterCard) as a replacement for the existing SSL standard. It provides a combination of a secure channel, electronic bank account and credit agency. It has been touted as the way forward for several years and in many ways it's a better way to transfer payment details, but it has yet to be adopted widely.

To use SET, customers need to register with a central agency. In exchange for their bank account details, each customer gets a unique certificate number. If a customer now wants to buy something online, they hand over proof of this unique certificate (rather than the certificate itself) to the shop, which in turn passes the proof on to the central agency that debits the customer's bank account. The key advantage is that the actual bank details are never transmitted and, thanks to clever encryption systems, nor is the customer's certificate. The problem is that SET is complex to install. Early trials proved disappointingly slow for shops and consumers, but it is likely that SET will start to gain ground over the next few years as a way of providing secure payments.

---

Some of the bigger portals, such as Yahoo!, offer a middle ground for consumers: they can store their credit-card details online within what they call a wallet. When they want to buy something (at a compatible shop), they type in their unique wallet ID. Another alternative is called eCharge. Consumers pay for goods by charging the amount to their telephone bill. This is great if you don't have a credit card, but it's of limited use otherwise.

Lastly, there are new virtual currencies that try to replace 'money' altogether. For example, Beenz (www.beenz.com) lets you collect points just by visiting sites or spending money; you can then pay for goods with your new Beenz currency.

## //ADDRESS BOOK

### Shopping carts

**Actinic Catalog**                                      **www.actinic.com**
Design and develop your shop on a desktop, then move it to your web server.

**Cart32**                                               **www.cart32.com**
Lots of features, but still easy to use and install. However, it only works on web servers running Windows.

**Cat@log 2.0**                                 **www.thevisionfactory.com**
Powerful, highly integrated and expensive commerce software from, unusually, a European company.

**CheckOut! Pro**                                        **www.n2plus.com**
Commerce software that's packed with stacks of options, but you can't deal with the manufacturers direct: you'll need to work with a development partner.

**COWS**                                                 **www.cows.co.uk**
Comprehensive, Perl-based software – developed in the UK but works with both UK and US credit card clearing companies.

**Dansie Shopping Cart**  www.dansie.net

Unusually, for Perl-based software, this system can be installed by a non-programmer and it runs on just about any standard web server.

**EasyCart**  www.easycart.com

Fill in some forms and you've got a shop. Just about one of the easiest ways to create a basic online store.

**FreeMerchant**  www.freemerchant.com

It's all free to set up – a complete, friendly and useful environment in which to house your online shop. All the charges are built into the transaction costs.

**IBM**  www.ibm.com/software/
**Net.Commerce**  webservers/commerce/

Comprehensive, powerful solutions for serious players with serious money to spend on development.

**iCat**  www.icat.com

One of the best-known products on the market. Either buy its feature-packed software to run on your server or create a shop on their server for a monthly fee. If you've less than ten items to sell, it's free.

**InterShop**  www.intershop.com

One of the best-established and most powerful, feature-laden shopping cart software packages around, and it can be configured to manage even the most demanding range of goods and services.

**JShop Pro**  www.jshop.co.uk

Be different. Clever programming allows this shopping software to run on the user's browser as JavaScript commands. And it's British.

**JumboStore**  www.jumbostore.com

Build a shop, process credit cards, even (very unusually) organise fulfilment – and the basic package is free.

**Mercantec SoftCart**  www.mercantec.com

Competing with InterShop at the top of the features table,

SoftCart is well known and supported by web design companies as a solution for complex online shops.

**Miva Merchant**                                    www.miva.com
Stacks of features, but your ISP needs to run special software before you can create a shop.

**PerlShop**                                    www.arpanet.com
Free Perl software that'll work in most situations – but you'll need to be confident with Perl, and your shop has to display a special logo.

**SalesCart**                                    www.salescart.com
One of the few programs that you can use if your website's designed with Microsoft FrontPage.

**ShopCreator**                                www.shopcreator.com
They promise that you can create an entire online store within fifteen minutes. Perhaps a little optimistic, but it's certainly quick and easy to use their templates to produce a working shop with your products hosted on their website.

**VIPCart**                                    www.vipcart.com
Forget programming problems. This free system lets you create and design a working online shop on a dedicated server.

**VirginBiz**                                    www.virginbiz.net
Follow the easy step-by-step instructions on their website and you'll end up with your own online shop. It's quick and simple, hosted on the VirginBiz server and paid for with a monthly fee scaled according to the number of products for sale. Best of all, there's masses of advice and tips on e-commerce and marketing online to make your site a success.

**Yahoo! Store**                            http://store.yahoo.com
Become part of the Yahoo! mall, where your monthly fee lets you create a shop that runs on the Yahoo! server.

## Payment processing

*There are hundreds of companies who can provide credit card processing services. You'll normally need an Internet merchant account from your bank, and a separate account with American Express if you want to accept their card. It can take up to six weeks to get an Internet merchant account from your bank. Your choice of company will probably be limited by whether they work with your shopping cart software and your bank. Ask your bank and choose your cart software first, then decide on the processing company. Almost all charge a fee on transactions – compare their rates at ShopForRates (www.shopforrates.com).*

### UK processing:

| | |
|---|---|
| **Secure Trading** | www.securetrading.com |
| **Datacash** | www.datacash.com |
| **NetBanx** | www.netbanx.co.uk |
| **WorldPay** | www.worldpay.com |

### US processing:

| | |
|---|---|
| **1st American card Service** | www.1stamericancardservice.com |
| **Advantage Merchant Services** | www.creditcardprocessor.com |
| **American Express** | www.americanexpress.com/business |
| **Authorize.Net** | www.authorize.net |
| **BankAmerica Merchant Services** | www.bankamerica.com |
| **Charge.Com** | www.charge.com |
| **Creditnet** | www.creditnet.com |
| **Electronic Payment Processing** | www.eppinc.com |
| **ePayments Resource Center** | www.epaynews.com |
| **GORealtime** | www.gorealtime.com |
| **iTransact** | www.redicheck.com |
| **Mastercard Merchant Site** | www.mastercard.com/merchants |
| **OpenMarket** | www.openmarket.com |
| **Pay2See.com** | www.pay2see.com |
| **Paylinx.com** | www.paylinx.com |

## SSL

*Find out more about the standard that's used to create most secure websites.*

**Netscape's                                   http://home.netscape.com/
SSL Page                                       security/techbriefs/ssl.html**
Everything you need to know about SSL security and how it all works.

**Planet SSL                                                www.rsa.com/ssl**
Information, advice, and answers about SSL.

**Security and                                   www.cs.auckland.ac.nz/
Encryption Links                               ~pgut001/links.html**
Links to just about every security website you'll need.

**VeriSign                                               www.verisign.com**
Want an SSL certificate? This is one of the best-known issuing companies: complete the application form, submit proof of your company's name and pay the yearly maintenance fee. A similar service is available from Thawte (**www.thawte.com**) – both offer the same end result for roughly the same price.

## SET

*The premature death of credit cards and SSL was predicted when the Secure Electronic Transaction standard was launched a few years ago. It's still not in widespread use but it does provide a model of future payment methods that will, eventually, be integrated into all web-access software to make shopping and online payments easier and more secure.*

**Secure Electronic Transaction                         www.setco.org**
What's happening in the fab, groovy world of SET – with an FAQ to answer all your many questions.

**SET Sites**                                    **www.SET-Sites.com**

So you've installed SET software – here's a directory of online merchants that currently support SET.

**Visa**                                          **www.visa.com**

One of the developers of SET explains how it compares with credit cards for online purchasing, and it lists shops that accept SET.

---

## The future of cash

---

*See what's going to happen to the coins and notes in your wallet. These are some of the sites that will bring you up to speed on digital developments – but be warned: the dry technical details and banking jargon can be indigestible.*

**DigiCash**                                      **www.digicash.com**

One of the pioneers of digital cash provides masses of news, guides and technology articles on the future of money.

**FAQ on**                          **http://ganges.cs.tcd.ie/mepeirce/**
**digital cash**                       **Project/Mlists/minifaq.html**

Concise answers to those nagging questions about the money that exists only as a series of 0s and 1s.

**National Electronic Commerce**                      **www.ecrc.**
**Resource Center**                                    **ctc.com**

Organisation with a mission to promote awareness of e-commerce and digital cash.

**Yahoo!**                    **www.yahoo.com/Business_and_Economy/**
**Electronic_Commerce/Digital_Money/**

Yahoo's selection of the main sites covering digital money, its future and implementation.

---

## Consumer complaints

---

*If your customers have a complaint with you, your service or goods, they'll try and resolve it directly with your company.*

*If you're convinced you are right, they could take their grievance to an online intermediary such as iLevel or the Internet Consumer Assistance Bureau. Visit these sites to see what you should do to avoid and resolve complaints without arbitration and get general advice on improving customer relations.*

**Advertising Standards Association**      **www.asa.org.uk**
Complaints about false advertising or claims in the UK.

**iLeveL**      **www.ilevel.com**
Helps to sort out problems between Internet shopper and shop.

**Internet Consumer Assistance Bureau**      **www.isitsafe.com**
Middle ground between consumer complaints and merchant responses.

**National Association of**      **www.nacab.**
**Citizens' Advice Bureaux**      **org.uk**
Will help lodge a complaint and work with you to resolve a consumer dispute with a supplier within the UK or the EU.

**Office of Fair Trading**      **www.oft.gov.uk**
Does not normally deal with consumer complaints but its site provides plenty of help for consumers. It can step in to help deal with recurrent problems.

**Trading Standards**      **www.tradingstandards.gov.uk**
This government body has the power to investigate claims against false service or supply of goods and is often used by consumers who've been scammed by an online shop.

---

#### Watchdogs

---

*There are plenty of websites that work for the consumer, providing lists of online shops that don't deliver what they promise or that treat consumers badly. Most also have lists of friendly shops that are recommended. Visit these to see what to do, and what not to do, to keep on their good side.*

**Bad, Better and Best**                           www.webBbox.com
**Businesses Bulletin Board**
Database of who's good and bad in the world of e-commerce.

**Better Business Bureau**                           www.bbb.org
Help for businesses that want to be good and for consumers that
want to complain. If you've a shop, apply to get into their directory
of nice people to do business with.

**BizRate**                                    www.bizrate.com
If you've annoyed a customer, here's where they might write a
report giving everyone else the low-down on the low life of e-
commerce.

**Internet Advocacy Center**           www.consumeradvocacy.com
Lots of useful stuff about fraud on the net.

**National Fraud Information Center**           www.fraud.org
Hear about frauds as they happen – geared to reporting US
fraudsters.

**Public Eye**                    www.thepubliceye.com/review.htm
Rates consumer sites of all kinds.

**Web Assurance Bureau**                    www.wabureau.com
Don't end up in here. This agency keeps archives of who's done
what, so consumers can tell the goodies from the baddies.

# 5//MARKETING ON THE INTERNET

With the Internet you get a whole new range of marketing tools to help promote your company, brand or range of products. In addition to traditional direct mail, display advertising and press relations, you now have powerful new features such as direct email, banner advertising and net-based press releases.

In this chapter we'll show you how to use the Internet to improve and enhance your marketing and PR activities for your existing brand or range of products and how to market your website.

## //DIRECT EMAIL MARKETING

One of the simplest, but most powerful, ways of marketing over the net is to send targeted email messages to customers (or potential customers). Since every user has a unique email address, and their email messages pop straight on to their desktop, it's a great way to reach users. Unfortunately, every other company has also thought of this and users can get fed up with email marketing – just as they are fed up with junk mail through the post.

To get lists of email addresses, you can gather the addresses yourself (see box below) or rent a list from a specialist list broker. Make sure that the names and addresses on the lists are 'opt-in' users (see below) and the broker is a member of a direct mail trade organisation.

If you follow the simple rules outlined below, you'll find direct email marketing is an effective way to streamline regular delivery of information such as:

- informing existing customers of new updates or promotions;
- gaining new customers through a cold-call mailshot;
- improving relations with existing customers via a regular newsletter;

- sending out regular sales information to distributors and your sales team;
- sending press releases to a list of journalists.

The entire direct email concept was spoilt early on by heavy-handed companies sending out millions of unsolicited messages to random, unknown users to promote their products. This almost always backfires and simply generates a lot of flame (hate mail) messages coming back to your company. However, if you use direct email carefully, with users who have agreed to accept advertising mail message delivery, then it's efficient, fast and very cheap.

---

**Recording email addresses**

One of the best ways to build an email list of people interested in your products is to ask them! Add a form feature to your website that lets visitors type in their email address and so receive regular updates, newsletters or special offers. If that's too difficult, ask them on your normal paper order forms.

---

Unsolicited mass mailings have a justifiably terrible reputation; these are the ones to avoid. This type of mailshot involves sending out tens or hundreds of thousands of messages to unknown people – the ultimate in cold calling. The trouble is that the recipients have not asked for the message and will probably delete it immediately. Some will reply with a flame message and very, very few will actually bother reading the contents. There are plenty of companies who will offer to supply a database file with millions of email addresses, but rent one and you'll be guaranteed to do more damage to your company's reputation than good.

A semi-research mailshot is a little better than a mass mailing, but only just. You can acquire email addresses from a whole range of places on the net: from newsgroup postings, mailing list messages or even chat sessions. If you want to tell users about your new brand of home-smoked cheese, you could look at the newsgroup postings in the alt.food newsgroups and subscribe to mailing lists about gourmet food. However, no-one's going to appreciate having their email addresses copied and used in this way.

If you send an advertising message to people who have specifically said that they are willing to receive messages about a particular product or industry, it's called an opt-in mailing. It's by far the best in terms of response and profile. Most of the reputable companies that rent out mailing lists will offer opt-in lists, where the names have been gathered through other websites.

**Mailing lists to rent**
Make sure that the list you're renting is opt-in – that the people on it have explicitly said that they users don't mind receiving unsolicited mail. Try these specialist email list brokers:

| | |
|---|---|
| **Copywriter** | **www.copywriter.com/lists** |
| **InBox Express** | **www.inboxexpress.com** |
| **PostMasterDirect** | **www.postmasterdirect.com** |
| **Targ-it** | **www.targ-it.com** |

## //PRESS RELATIONS

Almost all reporters have an email address, so it takes little imagination to realise that you could, potentially, deliver your press releases to key journalists instantly using email. In fact, many journalists prefer receiving releases by email because it's up to date and convenient – they can look at it in their own time rather than being browbeaten by PR folk over the telephone – and it doesn't add to the pile of paper cluttering their desks. By using a specialist agency, you can outsource a lot of mundane press work to a virtual agency that can provide coverage for a specific niche or country, or inform a global list of reporters who might be interested in your subject area.

As well as sending press releases, you can use the net to provide background information for journalists. Include an area on your website that has company briefings, product reviews, direct links to marketing contacts, historical documents and even the company's published financial details to help a journalist doing their research.

The web has produced a range of specialist press sites, such as the vast PR Newswire (**www.prnewswire.com**), which provide private forums allowing reporters to request information from companies for research into a story or feature. If you want to participate, and so get the chance of being used in a story or quoted by a journalist, you'll have to pay a subscription to include your company and product details.

Each web agency can provide different lists of journalists with special interests – and they all charge in different ways. Try these main sites to get an idea of what's on offer.

| | |
|---|---|
| **BusinessWire** | **www.businesswire.com** |
| **GINA** | **www.gina.com** |
| **Internet News Bureau** | **www.newsbureau.com** |
| **PRNewsTarget** | **www.newstarget.com** |
| **PRNewswire** | **www.prnewswire.com** |
| **URLwire** | **www.urlwire.com** |
| **Xpress Press** | **www.xpresspress.com** |

## //ADVERTISING

Advertising on the web has become another way of promoting a product or service, complementing traditional media such as print, TV, radio and direct mail. Just about every successful website is now peppered with long, thin banner advertisements, tempting users to click and be transported to a site on offer. The Internet advertising model seems near perfect – you can target your ads so that they are displayed to just a chosen section of viewers, selected by country of origin or subject of interest. Some of the most sophisticated advertising sites are the large, popular search engines (such as Yahoo! and Excite!). Here, advertisers can choose to display a banner ad triggered by a search keyword typed in by a user. If a visitor searches for plumbing suppliers, they'll get the results of the search plus banner ads from plumbing supply companies.

---

### Banner Standards

The size of banner advert panels has settled into two main standard sizes: 468 x 60 pixels or (sometimes) 100 x 75 pixels. Banners are normally stored as GIF or JPEG format image files and are created using a standard image or paint program. Within the banner's space you can design almost anything – and include a photograph, text, drawings or animation. Animated banner ads are created by drawing several images, all slightly different, which are then displayed in rapid succession. See the Address Book for websites specialising in banner ad designs.

---

A banner ad is normally hyperlinked to another site – if the advert catches a viewer's attention, they can click on it to jump to the advertiser's site. Because of this, they are particularly suited to advertising other websites, but you can use them to promote any special offer, product or service.

Many of the banner advertisements you see are brokered by vast, powerful online ad companies such as DoubleClick (**www.doubleclick.com**). They monitor which ads are displayed, how the customers are charged and the clients paid.

### The costs of banner adverts

Commercial websites will normally charge to display your banner advertisement. There's a whole range of different schemes used to charge for essentially the same service. There are two key terms to remember when comparing the costs of advertising: 'impression' and 'click-through'. When a banner advertisement is shown on a web page to a user, this is called an impression. When a banner advertisement is displayed on a web page and a user clicks on it, and is then transferred to another website, this is called a click-through. Most sites will charge you per impression, often termed CPM (cost per thousand impressions) or CPI (cost per impression). Paying by impression is fine if you want to display your message, but if you want to pay by result, try and get a click-through advertising rate, often termed CPA (cost per action).

Most websites that accept banner ads have a range of charges based on where on their site you want the ad displayed. CPM rates normally range from £14 ($20) to £140 ($200) per thousand times that your ad is displayed. CPA rates are often far, far higher and generally subject to much negotiation.

Before you set aside an advertising budget for web-based banner ads, it's worth measuring the conversion rates of this media. If your banner ad is shown one thousand times, what sort of click-through response should you expect? Normally, you'll be lucky to average a 1 or 2% CTR (click-through rate) and, as users get bored with banner ads, this percentage keeps dropping. However, if you have a specific product to offer and target your adverts to specialist websites, you can easily improve the CTR up to a maximum of 8-10%.

Unfortunately for the advertisers, the reality is that a lot of surfers ignore the ads; many find them intrusive and irritating and, for those that feel strongly on the issue, there's special software that'll strip out ads before they are ever displayed. One of the main complaints from the users is that they take time to download and slow down the surfing experience. Many marketing industry commentators note that, on a per-viewer basis, the ad rates for a tiny banner image on a website are just as expensive as a full-page, colour ad in a popular magazine.

### Free banner advertising
If you've no budget for banner advertising, you can still get your banner ad displayed on hundreds of other sites using one of the

many free banner exchange cooperatives, such as LinkExchange (www.linkexchange.com). See the Address Book for a list of similar services. The catch is that you have to accept other people's ads on your site in return – and often you've no idea what type of advert you'll have to display.

### Branding

The net is a great place for fast brand marketing. In many areas, it's the first company off the blocks with the best brand awareness that wins the customer loyalty. For example, if you ask surfers for an online bookshop, they'll probably respond with Amazon (www.amazon.com). Similarly, choose a search engine and you'll probably hear Yahoo! (www.yahoo.com). These companies benefited from the lack of competition in the early development days of the net. Now, you'll have to work hard to build brand awareness on the web – especially since you'll be up against the vast million-dollar budgets of the new launches to the stock market.

Many companies create a separate brand just for the Internet. It might sound hip or cool, have a wacky name and appeal to the core net population. For example, US bookselling giant Barnes and Noble has changed its online brand away from 'barnesandnoble.com' to a sleeker 'bn.com'. So did successful magazine publisher Ziff Davis, which now owns the 'zdnet.com' range of popular sites covering computer news and features.

Creating a new brand on the Internet can, compared to the traditional business model, be very fast. Within a few months of it starting, most people in the UK had heard of Freeserve (the ISP), and the vast valuations placed on hi-tech Internet start-up companies means that they have a huge marketing budget available.

## //RESEARCH AND FOCUS GROUPS

If you are planning a new product or campaign, it's worth testing out the theory on a small, select (but representative) group of people. They'll soon tell you if your choice of colour, price or name is great or daft. Using old-fashioned business models, this process was often used only by the biggest companies, which could afford to hire teams of market research staff and wait weeks for the results. Use one of the new instant-response marketing companies based on the Internet and you'll get the thoughts of hundreds or thousands of selected viewers within minutes – and at a far lower cost. One of the biggest of these companies is Greenfield Online (**www.greenfield.com**).

Instead of using a marketing company to do this background research and response work for you, you can save money and do much of it yourself by careful – very careful – use of newsgroups (see page 97). Before you do this, make sure that you understand the ground rules – very few groups allow any sort of business message or product plug.

---

Newsgroups are sometimes used by journalists asking for feedback on a product or topic. You can also judge the viability of a potential new product by monitoring newsgroups for such requests.

---

Use the newsgroups as a way of listening to your customers, and potential contacts, for response to a product (your own or a rival's product). Many of the newsgroups are job- or product-specific: find the newsgroups that match your company's interests and you can tap in to the opinions and thoughts of your target audience – use search engines such as Deja (**www.dejanews.com**) to find relevant newsgroups. Once you've identified a selection of newsgroups, make sure that someone in the company – preferably in your marketing department – keeps a daily watch on the messages, questions and complaints posted to the groups. By doing this, you can wage an effective, but low-key, PR campaign. Make sure that the experts in your company answer questions posed in newsgroups authoritatively. Don't turn your postings into an advertising message; instead, rely on a short signature at the end of each message to tell other readers about the company. This also works well as a way of defusing potential complaints and shows that the company is listening to its customers.

## //ADDRESS BOOK

### Email marketing

*If you're planning to drop a million emails to unsuspecting users promoting your new widget, don't. You'll get flamed with hate mail and damage your company's reputation. Instead, get a list from one of the reputable suppliers and take the good advice of trade organisations such as the DMA.*

**Alphasoft Net.Mailer**            **www.alphasoftware.com**
Clever software that replaces your email program for bulk mailshots.

**Arial Software Campaign**            **www.arialsoftware.com**
Software to help you manage your email list and post off the thousands of messages.

**Colorado Soft WorldMerge**            **www.coloradosoft.com**
Custom software that'll mail merge email address lists for a speedy way to send bulk mail.

**EverythingAbout**            **www.**
**Email resource site**            **everythingaboutemail.com**
As you'd guess, everything from software to advice, resources and lists for rent.

**MailKing**            **www.mailking.com**
Keeps you sane when managing bulk mailings.

**US Direct Marketing Association**            **www.the-dma.com**
Masses of good advice, and a code of conduct, to help prevent you blundering around upsetting people.

**Yahoo!**                           http://dir.yahoo.com/
                           Business_and_Economy/Companies/
                           Marketing_and_Advertising/Direct_Marketing/

Yahoo's directory is a good place to start looking for lists, software and ideas.

---

### Banner advertising

---

**Adbility.com**                           www.adbility.com

Everything you need to know about advertising on the web.

**AdBot.com**                           www.adbot.com

A great place to pick up cheap ads on the biggest websites. It auctions off unwanted ad space from the major portals at discount prices. It's fantastically busy and slow, but persevere.

**Adclub.net**                           www.adclub.net

Pay to place your banner ad, or get paid to accept ads on your site.

**Banneradnetwork.com**        www.banneradnetwork.com

One of the oldest free banner ad exchange programmes that helps get your site noticed.

**Bannerexchange.com**           www.bannerexchange.com

Free banner ad exchange service – place ads on your site and your ad will be displayed on other sites. An effective, cheap way to spread the word.

**Bannertips.com**                           www.bannertips.com

Masses of practical tips and advice about designing and placing banner ads.

**Bannerworkz.com**                    www.bannerworkz.com

Are you the world's worst artist? Or would you rather not try and design your banner yourself? If so, get your new banner ad designed here.

**Bcentral.com**                    www.bcentral.com
Stacks of useful tools and advice to help you promote your site –
including designing and placing ads. And all provided by Microsoft.

**Budget Banners**                www.budget-banners.com
Want a banner designed? Get one produced here for a low flat fee.

**Internet Link Exchange**            www.linkexchange.com
Just about the best-known banner ad exchange programme that'll
distribute your ad on other sites – for free.

**Outerplanet.com**                www.outerplanet.com
Discussion forum where you can post messages offering to buy or
sell banner advertising space on your site.

---

### Advertising agencies

*If you're planning to buy ad space on other sites, you could use an
online advertising agency to book and coordinate the campaign.
Similarly, if you're planning to sell ad space on your site, you can
use the same specialist agencies to broker the deals. Here are
some of the main players in the agency field.*

| | |
|---|---|
| DoubleClick | www.doubleclick.com |
| Ipro | www.ipro.com |
| Market Match | www.marketmatch,com |
| SoftBank Media | www.simweb.com |
| WebConnect | www.worlddata.com |
| WebTrack | www.webtrack.com |

# 6//PROMOTING YOUR SITE

Every day, thousands of new websites launch, so here's how to make sure your site gets noticed. There are dozens of different ways of promoting your site – using traditional marketing channels and through the Internet itself. As well as informing potential visitors, customers and press, you also have to tell the online search databases that you exist. It's these search engines, such as Yahoo! (**www.yahoo.com**) and Excite! (**www.excite.com**), that are the key to a high profile on the web.

## //ANNOUNCING YOUR WEBSITE

Here's a checklist of the things you should do to ensure that your new website gets maximum exposure. Do everything here and everyone that could know, will know. After this, it's down to the quality of the site – your products and content:

- Make sure all your web pages include indexing information.
- Submit your site to the main search engines.
- Submit your site to 'what's new' sites.
- Ask related and trade sites to exchange links.
- Change company advertising and stationery to include the website address.
- Make sure that your emails include a 'signature' at the bottom of your emails with your site's address.
- Consider banner advertising.
- Target traditional PR channels.
- Tell your key customers.

**The search engines**
The most important step in marketing your website is to make sure it's registered with the main search engines and directories. These

search engines carry an index of millions of websites, together with a short description and link to the site. You know how they work – you've probably used them to find a site. Type in a word and they will display any websites that match.

Most of the major search engines use automatic software robot programs, called spiders, to find new websites. These are then analysed and added automatically to the main index. You could wait for the spider to find your new site but, because there are so many new sites, it could take them weeks to reach yours. Sidestep the automatic system and register your site directly with the search engine (see below).

### Make your site search-engine friendly

To help the search engine correctly analyse and index your site, you can add special codes into the file that's used to store the web page. These codes, called meta-tags, are an extension to the HTML language (used to layout the page) and are only used for indexing – they're not displayed.

The meta-tags need to be added manually to each page. Most web design software lets you add these using a special form but if not, you will have to edit the text file that contains the web page – using Windows Notepad or a similar text editor. If you add the tags manually, they need to be in the first few lines of the file, within the <HEADER>...</HEADER> section.

First, type in the key words for the page (normally between a dozen and fifty words) that someone might type in at a search engine to find your site. These are used by the search engine to directly index the page. For example, if you sell pet supplies, you could use words such as 'cat, dog, bone, litter, collar' and so on. This entry would look like this:

```
<META NAME="KEYWORDS" CONTENT="cat, dog, bone,
litter, collar">
```

Next, you need to write a concise description of what's on the page. Don't write more than 30-40 words and make sure you include a clear description within the first few words. The search engine often displays this description if it matches a search by a user. If you don't include this description, the engine will use the first chunk of text it finds on the page. Here's what our pet shop might write:

```
<META NAME="DESCRIPTION" CONTENT="A vast range of
pet supplies that are cheap and delivered fast. Caring
advice from expert vets, special offers for furry, fishy or
feathered animals">
```

### Submit your site to search engines

Once you have prepared your website with meta-tags, you can submit it for indexing by the search engines. You can either do this manually by visiting each search engine site and completing a submission form online, or you can use a commercial service that will automatically submit your information to a range of sites. If you are in a hurry, use one of the automatic submission services such as SubmitIt (**www.submit-it.com**), Exploit (**www.exploit.com**), DidIt (**www.did-it.com**) or All4One (**www.all4one.com**). To keep a track of the different requirements of engines, visit the invaluable Search Engine Watch website (**www.searchenginewatch.com**).

---

Some search engines, notably Yahoo! (www.yahoo.com), use human editors to trim down and edit meta-tag page descriptions, so make sure that they meet the submission requirements.

---

### Online reviews and listings

Users like to know what's new on the web – and will often visit a new site if it looks interesting. This can be enough to spread the word that your site is worth a look. To this end, there are dozens of popular 'what's new' sites. These vary between a simple listing to comprehensive editorial reviews from a panel of experts. Some charge, but most are a free service and it's worth submitting your new site to each. And if the review panel think your site good enough, you could even get an award, and that will also help attract visitors.

The best place to start is Award Sites (**www.awardsites.com**) which lists over 2000 award and 'what's new' sites.

### Reciprocal links

To help publicise your site, send an email to the webmaster of other sites that cover the same subject and ask if they will add a link to your page. For example, if you supply classic car parts, see if you can be added as a link within websites for car clubs or garages specialising in restoration. If the subject's popular enough, there might be a web ring (a collection of sites linked together to help visitors move from one site to the next) that you could join. Visit other similar sites to see if they are part of a ring. If you ask another webmaster to add your site as a link, be prepared to add a link to their site to your page.

---

To remind colleagues of your website, make sure that your website address is in your email signature – the text that's added to the end of all email messages or newsgroup postings you send. All email software lets you create a signature (for example, in Microsoft IE choose Tools/Options/Signatures) that should be just a few lines long and include your name, company, motto and website address.

---

### Newsgroups and mailing lists

One of the best places to find potential visitors to your website is in the speciality newsgroups and mailing lists that cover your niche area of interest (see Chapter 8). Bear in mind that almost all newsgroups and mailing lists have a policy of no business messages. Read what the other members write and, if you can answer a question or provide information, do so – but without any blatant plugs for your company. Instead, leave it to your signature to tell others about your company.

---

**Banner advertising**
If your net budget has not been exhausted with design, content and staff, you could always run a banner advertisement campaign to promote your new site. See pages 66-68 for more details on the ways you can buy ad space on other commercial sites – or even get space for free.

---

### Measuring response and analysing visitors

An essential part of any website marketing effort is the ability to monitor who's visiting and what they've been doing on your site. There are simple counters (rather like a milometer) that advance each time a visitor arrives on your site. But these don't tell you much and can look amateurish. Instead, you should use access logs.

Access logs are set up by your website hosting company and record every click of every visitor to your site in minute, but inde-cipherable, detail. To make use of this data, you'll need to pour the access log data into a specialist program that will create tables, reports and pretty graphs. The information is invaluable and it should tell you:

- which country your visitors are from
- which products are of most interest to visitors
- if a special offer or new product is successful
- where your visitors were before they reached you
- the success of your banner ad or email campaign.

---

Use access log analysis to find out where visitors were before they came to your site. Contact the most popular referrer – if it's not a competitor – and see if you can add exchange links or banner adverts or even create a special discount or offer for your products that's then advertised on their website.

A more advanced stage of monitoring visitors involves trying to predict what they would like to see. Many of the biggest websites use sophisticated software to trace what a visitor does when on your site and then display relevant material or adverts that might be of interest. For example, if someone on Excite! (www.excite.com) checks the weather in Chicago, tracking software at Excite! will spot this and start to display banner ads from services in the city.

## //ADDRESS BOOK

### Promoting to search engines

*Save loads of time by using special software that automatically submits your site to hundreds of search engines – but you'll probably have to pay for the privilege. And to keep up to date with changes, visit SearchEngineWatch (www.searchenginewatch.com).*

**All4One**                                      www.all4one.com
Automatically submit your website to 20 top search engines – free.

**DidIt**                                        www.did-it.com
Pay a fee and get expert help promoting your site to search engines – and they offer a service to refresh the search engines with details of your site.

**Exploit**                                      www.exploit.com
Will automatically submit your new site to hundreds of search engines and directories. There's a cut-down version that's free – try and visit the main search sites yourself (see Chapter 7 for a list), then use this as a free extra.

**LinkPopularity**                              www.linkpopularity.com
Try this one a few weeks after publicising your site to see who else has linked to your site – always a good guide to how well you're

doing. As a simpler alternative, search for your website's address in AltaVista (www.altavista.com) using the key word 'link:' (as in 'link:virgin.com' to see who links to the Virgin site) for one engine's view of your site.

**SearchEngineWatch**                    **www.searchenginewatch.com**
Find out how different search engines work and how to submit your site to their indexes.

**SubmitIt**                              **www.submit-it.com**
The oldest and still the best service that'll submit your site to hundreds of search engines – for a fee. If you want to make do with the top ten search engines, SubmitIt will do this job for free.

**WebPosition**                           **www.webposition.com**
Tells you how your site is listed and ranked with the top search engines.

---

### What's new and award sites

*Proud of your site? Submit it to one of the guides that cover new websites and you might be reviewed or listed. You could even get an award – all help to drive visitors to your site. Don't forget that most hi-tech newspapers and magazines, such as USA Today (www.usatoday.com), also have listings for new sites.*

**Award Sites**                           **www.awardsites.com**
Lists over 2000 award and 'what's new' sites – the best place to start.

**Internet Magazine**    **www.Internet-magazine.com/bookmarks**
The UK's leading Internet magazine lists the new, cool and newsworthy sites.

**Netscape**          **www.netscape.com/netcenter/new.html**
High-traffic site tells you what are new and cool sites according to Netscape.

**Yahoo!**                                **www.yahoo.com/picks**
The editors at Yahoo! choose their top new sites for the week.

## Measuring response and web analysis

*Ask your web-hosting provider to supply access logs; these carry detailed information about every click and move of each visitor to your site. You'll need a web log analysis product to produce meaningful information from the access logs. Before you buy, ask your hosting provider – some supply free analysis software.*

**Accrue Software**                    www.accrue.com
Comprehensive, high-end log analysis software that can help you track visitors and trends in their behaviour when on your site.

**Analog**                www.statslab.cam.ac.uk/~sret1/analog
Just about the most-used log analyser, but it can be fiddly to install and you should be comfortable with Perl.

**Aptex**                    www.aptex.com
High-power software that's packed with features – as used by leading commerce sites like Amazon.com.

**DoubleClick**                    www.doubleclick.com
Monster web-based ad agency provides geo-targeting and complex customer analysis tools.

**GeoSys mapping**                    www.geosys.com
You're from where? Powerful software to map customers to regions.

**WebTrends**                    www.webtrends.com
Friendly, detailed web analysis tells you who visited, when and what they did – ideal for small- to medium-sized sites.

**Yahoo!**            http://dir.yahoo.com/Computers_and_Internet/
Software/Internet/World_Wide_Web
There are hundreds of competing products, some free, some expensive, some terrible. A good place to start exploring is Yahoo's directory.

# 7//SEARCHING

The Internet can bring you everything you could ever want to know, and quite a lot of things that you don't. And the biggest problem is how to find what you're looking for within the mass of information available. The Internet contains information of use to every business, large or small. Here are some of the things you can find:

- Information about airlines, financial organisations, governments, reference and much more.
- News from almost every area – from world headlines to niche business news.
- Economic indicators, theories and forecast information.
- Real-time information: pages that update their contents every few seconds (such as a share price).
- Static background information, such as annual reports or dictionaries.
- Databases of historical newspaper and magazine articles that are archived and searchable.
- Databases with historical company results and share information.
- Articles providing advice and expertise on everything from start-ups to export markets.
- Places to trade surplus stock.
- Online shops where you can buy everything from office furniture to machinery – often at a discount.
- Discussion groups where you can ask for opinions, chat about products or services or get feedback.

Much of the information is maintained by knowledgeable enthusiasts or respected companies, but there's plenty written by amateurs whose information may not be accurate and reliable. Stick to the established sources and you'll avoid the dross and contentious outpourings of millions of opinionated users at the risk of missing out on the fun of the net. And best of all, almost all the information on the Internet is free to search and display – there are a few services that charge, but this is very unusual.

In this chapter, we cover the ways you can search the web to find the nugget of information in a website or newsgroup. For a selection of the best sites, flip to the directory section on page 206, where we feature hundreds of websites that cover everything from government statistics to marine equipment, organised neatly into sections.

## //SEARCHING FOR BUSINESS INFORMATION

The Internet provides two basic types of information source. First is the web; it contains millions of websites that provide everything from company reports to business magazine features. Some websites include vast databases to offer archived material, historical analysis and information; others contain just a few pages of text. Second are transient discussion groups, such as news-groups, that provide a free-for-all forum in which anything can be discussed. Both are useful for business research.

If you are searching for information, researching a new project or after advice, most people head straight for the web, but newsgroups and mailing lists are great if you want to listen to real people talking and complaining about products – they could be your products.

But how do you find what you want? With millions of web pages out there, you'll need plenty of help to hunt out a site that's relevant. We've compiled some of the best and most useful business sites in Chapter 9 but, in a book of this size, we can't include everything – so, if you want to find other information, you'll need to use the online search tools.

**Where to start**

One of the best places to start looking for business information is at one of the business megasites, also known as portals. Some are based around well-known business magazines, such as Inc. (**www.inc.com**), Fortune (**www.fortune.com**) or Fast Company (**www.fastcompany.com**); others are just information portals that gather together data from hundreds of other specialist business sites. They often repackage information – for example, company news and results – from other organisations, or provide useful directories that have direct links to relevant sites. You'll find a great selection of some of the top business portals at the start of the main directory (Chapter 9).

To help find a web page that contains information about what you want to know, you'll need to use a search site – one whose sole job is to provide an index of other website addresses listed according to key words and descriptions in the original page. Type in a word or phrase and you'll see a list of websites and their addresses that match your search request. As usual, the Internet provides plenty of choice, with hundreds of different sites that help you find other relevant sites and information.

As you browse the web, you'll soon find that there are hundreds of directories of business sites, mostly part of a larger general search engine. Some of the biggest directories are provided by the major portal sites such as Yahoo!, Excite!, Lycos and MSN, but you'll find a great range of businesses in specialist business directories such as BizWeb (**www.bizweb.com**) – it might be sparse on design, but it's packed with links. Business portals and magazine sites generally link to, or contain, a limited number of links to other sites. This means you could miss out on some of the more obscure sites.

A better way to hunt out your specialist site is to use your favourite general-purpose search engine such as Excite! or Lycos – or, better still, use a metasearch tool. Don't bother hiking from one general-purpose search engine to another: let the metasearcher do the legwork for you. Just type in your question and the metasearch site will automatically submit the question to all the main search engines and directories, then filter the answers for relevance and present you with a manageable list. Sites like Google, DogPile, All-in-One and MetaCrawler offer the benefit of all the search engines without the bother of visiting each one.

And if you prefer your information filtered and reviewed, look to the directories that use a real live human editor to manage the sections. Sites such as LookSmart (**www.looksmart.com**) and About (**www.about.com**), go one step further than plain directories like Excite! or Lycos. They have editors who write mini reviews of each site together with useful guides to the subject – whether it's accounting practice or direct marketing techniques. These are great for surfers who prefer to trust the word of a fellow human being, but it does limit the range of sites stored in the directory.

**Power searching**
Whatever kind of search you do, you won't want thousands of hobby or enthusiast sites cluttering up the search results. A simple search for 'broker' will display thousands of hits to everything from yacht-brokers to power-brokers. To limit the results you see, you'll need to start using the 'power' search features that are part of all search engines and will help you refine your search. These usually work by filtering selections through one or more different criteria, defined by 'search expressions'.

To see how to improve your search technique, zip over to the friendliest search engine, HotBot (**www.hotbot.com**). You can quickly and easily define a complex search expression by choosing words that must or must not be matched. Simply click on the pull-down menus to create your search expression: it's really very easy to specify a complicated search that finds sites offering business advice on problems with export to Japan, but not sites about travel to Japan.

If HotBot is not your usual search engine, you will have to use a rather less friendly notation system to refine your queries. Almost all the search engines, including Yahoo! and Excite!, let you refine your query using '+' and '-' symbols. If you put a '+' sign in front of a word, it means the word must be matched. And the '-' works in just the opposite way. So our previous query would be entered as 'advice +export +Japan -travel'.

Some search engines prefer to use Boolean operators (the words AND, OR, NOT, usually in capitals), but these work in a similar way to the '+' and '-' signs used in Excite! and Yahoo! For example, with Boolean logic, our example would read 'advice AND export AND Japan NOT travel'.

As you sift through your results, you'll soon realise that the search engine is looking for all your words in any order on the web page. The next step to power status is to match an exact expression. If you want to search for a particular phrase, enclose the words within single quote marks. For example, if you want to find sites covering employee benefits you should enclose the two words within quotes: 'employee benefits'.

---

Government sites often have stacks of useful, if rather dull, information. For example, the British Council (www.britcoun.org) is packed with profiles of potential export targets and background information on countries.

---

**Finding similar sites**
A quick, neat and free way of adding a little zing to your web searches is to use a built-in feature of the latest browsers. When you've found a site you like, click on the 'Options/Show Related Sites' menu or 'What's related' button to see a list of sites covering the same subject. Unfortunately, it relies on a central database that knows how to link to different sites, and it works only some of the time.

The technology behind this trick is called Alexa. You can download a more powerful version of the same software, which works with any browser. It installs itself as a tiny icon on the status bar at the bottom of the browser window. Download a free copy from **www.alexa.com**.

---

Don't spend hours flicking between different supplier sites hunting down the cheapest price – let the web do the work for you. Use a specialist price search site, such as ShopSmart (www.shopsmart.com) or MySimon (www.mysimon.com) to find the source of the lowest prices for books, computers, software, music and videos.

---

**Problems and pitfalls**

The Internet is a vast, very useful library, but there are a few problems and pitfalls to beware – especially if you plan to base a business decision on your net research. Well-known publications and news sources, such as *The Economist* (**www.economist.com**) and the *Financial Times* (**www.ft.com**) have teams of editors, reporters and researchers who all ensure that the material is checked and accurate. The same is not always true of Fred's Secrets of Business Success or other hobby sites. It's sometimes difficult to know if an article you're reading is drawn from a published journal or is an offbeat thesis from a renegade student. Stick to the ideal of only basing important business decisions on information you can trust – it's true in the real world and even more so on the net.

The second problem is that you can easily spend more time trying to find information via the Internet than if you used your usual sources. Just because you have a connection to the Internet doesn't mean that you have to use it. If you have a good relationship with your bank, accountant or lawyer, they will probably be able to help with simple questions over the phone, and the telephone remains in many ways the best way to research your competitors and the market.

# //ADDRESS BOOK

## Finding a business

*B2B, or business to business, is the next big thing for the Internet – but trying to find another web-friendly business that displays products on its website and accepts orders and payment online can be difficult. To help track down a spanner manufacturer or a specialist wholesaler, use one of the many specialist business directories that list thousands of companies, organised neatly into categories.*

**1st Global Directory**    www.123link.com/main/1stglobal.html
Too many worldwide companies to contemplate – the individual categories alone number 17,000.

**555-1212.com Directory**    www.555-1212.com
Good directory of local and national, mostly US, companies.

**A Source**    www.asource.com
Avoid paper; find a partner company that claims to be e-friendly.

**BizExpose.com**    www.bizexposure.com
Stacks of companies and where you can find them on the net.

**BizWeb**    www.bizweb.com
A sparse but useful directory of over 40,000 companies on the web.

**Business Seek**    www.businesseek.com
Find the right company by name, product or industry.

**ComFind Business Search**    http://comfind.com
Global reach to this mammoth directory of companies online.

**CommerceInc**    http://search.commerceinc.com
Want millions of US companies? They're here.

**Companies House**    www.companieshouse.org.uk
Direct access to the UK database of registered companies – oddly, for an online database, it's only open during normal business hours.

**CompaniesOnline**  www.companiesonline.com
Mini profiles of US companies, from credit agency Dun and Bradstreet.

**Dot Com Directory**  www.dotcomdirectory.com
The official company that registers new domain names reverses its database to create an invaluable directory of companies and websites.

**Dow-Jones**  http://businessdirectory.
**Business Directory**  dowjones.com
Big brand, big directory. Stacks of sections that include links to companies online as well as guides to all aspects of business, jobs, finance, government and small business.

**EcoMall Companies**  www.ecomall.com/biz
Find a company that's eco-friendly and has a website.

**Enterprise Zone**  www.enterprisezone.org.uk
Links and advice to help you find the UK business resource you're looking for online.

**ExpertFind**  www.expertfind.com
Find an accountant or other expert in your local US state.

**Export Hotline Online**  www.exporthotline.com
Cross barriers; search this directory of companies that are dedicated to import and export.

**FirstList Mergers and Acquisitions**  www.firstlist.com
Don't just find a business, buy one. Here's a directory of online companies for sale.

**GovWorks**  www.govworks.com
Find the US government department that does what you need.

**Grail Search**  www.grailsearch.com
Improve your international relations – stacks of resources, advice, profiles and a directory of companies in each country.

### Greatinfo.Com        www.greatinfo.com
The usual vast directory of US companies, together with useful business columns, news, advice and features.

### Hoover's Online        www.hoovers.com
Extremely comprehensive directory of US companies, with tables of the biggest, fastest growing and most important.

### IndustryLink        www.industrylink.com
Aerospace, manufacturing, electronics, chemicals – there are thousands of companies listed in this database of industrial companies online

### Information Please        http://infoplease.looksmart.com
Find that company or read the huge, assorted collection of business advice and resources.

### IntelliSearch        www.intellisearchnow.com
Gathers together over 1,500 business sources and directories, and charges you to search them.

### Minority Business Directory        www.mbnet.com
Directory of companies owned or managed by ethnic and social minorities – that is, anyone except white males.

### NYSE – Listed Companies        www.nyse.com/listed/listed.html
If they're on the Street at the NYSE, they're listed here.

### onVia        www.onvia.com
Brilliant way of getting bids from online US and Canadian companies for just about anything, from direct mail to office furniture. The future of business deals has arrived.

### Pronet        www.pronet.ca
Where's that Canadian company?

### Rescue Island – Business Search        www.rescueisland.com
Claims it's the fountain of information for business websites – not quite true, but it's a good and plentiful source of useful business links.

**Standard & Poor's 500**    www.spglobal.com/500mainframe.html
The 500 companies, with profiles, that make up the S&P stock index.

**Starting Point Business Categories**         www.stpt.com
International directory of companies that's particularly good in legal and marketing fields.

**Startup Zone**                    www.startupzone.com
Contemplating a start-up? Here's where to find venture capital, e-commerce experts, lawyers, media and content providers.

**The Biz**                        www.thebiz.co.uk
Invaluable directory of business websites, each with a short description; great for finding a bank in Bahrain or a metal workshop in Manchester.

**Thomas Regional Directories**      www.thomasregional.com
Local US companies by region or state.

**TopStartups.com**                  www.topstartups.com
Follow the leaders – profiles of the top start-up companies and how they did it.

**VerticalNet**                      www.verticalnet.com
Only want to talk to furniture makers? Industry-specific directories and news mean that you can name your sector and find out lots about it.

**ZDNet Company Finder New!**  www.zdnet.com/companyfinder/
First, find your technology company from this impressive directory of thousands of sites.

---

### Search engines and directories

---

*Search engines and directories are one of the best ways of finding a website that covers a subject of interest. Search engines, such as AltaVista, try to list every site available on the web, whereas directories, such as Yahoo!, limit themselves to a select few thousand. To help you browse through the entries, the listings are usually organised into categories, so you can browse all the plumbers or do a general search for plumbing across all categories. Most of these sites now have a similar look and feel and all provide powerful, efficient ways of searching for relevant websites. The downside is that if you type in a search word such as 'printers' you might get hundreds – often hundreds of thousands – of matching sites. If you're really serious about your searching, check out the 'read me' sections at the search engine site for full details of how to get the best out of it.*

**About**  www.about.com
One person writes friendly, cosy but efficient guides to just about every subject area.

**AltaVista**  www.altavista.com
Boasts just about the biggest index on the web.

**Euroseek**  www.euroseek.net
Europhiles head for this multilingual, multicountry search engine.

**Excite!**  www.excite.co.uk
Part portal, part mammoth index that cleverly tries to find similar sites. Includes a directory to let you browse sites by category together with its own news, weather and financial pages.

**G.O.D.**  www.god.co.uk
British and proud of it! No frills, no messing, but often slow.

**HotBot**  www.hotbot.com
Just about the friendliest engine on the web. Has the usual news, weather and money features but, so far, there's no UK-specific search.

**Infoseek**  www.infoseek.com
The best all-round player.

**LookSmart**  www.looksmart.co.uk
Very easy to navigate, and each site gets a comment from an editor.

**Lycos**                              www.lycos.co.uk
The granddaddy of search engines, Lycos combines a good index with directories.

**Magellan**                              www.mckinley.com
Sites get a review and a star rating, but try elsewhere for general searches.

**Northern Light**                              www.northernlight.com
Vast, fast and accurate.

**Scoot**                              www.scoot.co.uk
Find your nearest accountant or IFA. Easy-to-use collection of local businesses from around the UK.

**UKPlus**                              www.ukplus.com
Find UK-specific sites in a hurry. Neatly organised with plenty of choice.

**WebCrawler**                              www.webcrawler.com
If it's out there, you'll probably find it here.

**Yahoo!**                              www.yahoo.com
One of the first and, for many users, still the best. Clearly organised sections with a vast range of extra goodies – news, weather, shopping, free email, and finance information. You might never want to leave. For country-specific versions, try adding your country's domain suffix as in: www.yahoo.co.uk.

**Yell**                              www.yell.co.uk
Not the easiest to use, but holds the full Yellow Pages, company sites and news.

---

**Metasearchers**

---

*Silly name for a good idea. These chaps will do all the hard work for you and submit your query to all the search engines and directories in one go – then return the top hits.*

**AllOneSearch**                    www.allonesearch.com
Digs through over 500 of the major search engines to try to find the morsel you're after.

**AskJeeves**                    www.askjeeves.com
Type in a question. The urbane Jeeves will try to find a site that answers it, but he does sometimes get the wrong end of the stick and come up with some odd suggestions.

**DogPile**                    www.dogpile.com
Hardly elegant sophistication, but a faithful friend for specific searches. It's strangely weak on UK sites.

**Google!**                    www.google.com
One of the best around, and it's particularly good at weeding out irrelevant results.

**InferenceFind**                    www.infind.com
Clean, clinical metasearcher that groups together sites by category, rather than by search engine.

**MetaCrawler**                    www.metacrawler.com
Returns a manageable selection of the top results from the major search engines.

**Savvy Search**                    www.savvysearch.com
Let this site take the strain of searching a couple of dozen of the top search engines.

# 8//DISCUSSING BUSINESS

To many users, the Internet means the web – glossy pictures, clever design and lots of information. Yes, there are thousands of websites that can help you devise a new business model, buy new equipment at auction or display graphs of a competitor's share price. But many business people just want to discuss things: about trading, profits, staff, growth, marketing, export, ideas, complaints, tips, strategies and worries. And the Internet is very good at bringing together groups of users. There are tens of thousands of different places where you can discuss just about any subject you can imagine – and many more besides.

If you want to discuss anything, you can visit three different types of forum that for many users form the real heart of the net. These are:

1   Web forums or discussion areas.

2   Mailing lists.

3   Newsgroups (also called Usenet).

For business chat, you'll probably find that the discussion groups that form part of business magazine and advice websites prove the most useful, but, to get the full effect of free speech, take a tour of the newsgroups.

There's nothing fancy about any of these discussion forums – they are the plain text-only cousins of the web. Somehow, this makes it an even more powerful medium for people to say just whatever they want. Sure, you'll find scraps of news and you can make friends, but it's mostly comment, opinions, rants, jobs, questions, thoughts, advice, for sale ads and all the other detritus that makes up normal life.

## //DISCUSSION GROUPS

Some of the most popular features of business magazine websites are their discussion groups. Most major business magazine sites – such as Inc. magazine (www.inc.com) – have a part of the site dedicated to discussion groups. Anyone can join in the discussion – although you may be asked to register first, for free. Each website has one group or more, each covering a particular theme. Together, the groups cover a wide range of topics, from marketing to hiring and firing. Some groups are very active; others are rather stagnant and not worth the visit.

Some web-based discussion groups originated back in the pre-Internet days of bulletin-board systems, such as CompuServe (www.compuserve.com), AOL (www.aol.com) and CIX (www.cix.co.uk). All three still offer a very wide range of discussion groups (called forums), but you can access them only if you're a subscriber.

When you visit a website with a discussion group, such as Fast Company (www.fastcompany.com/community/), you'll see a list of the titles of the previous few messages. To read a message, double-click on its title. If a message has a reply, it should display a tiny plus sign just to the left. Click on this and you'll see the original message and all the related replies. You can click on another button to add your own thoughts, or to reply to a message. A new web page is displayed; fill in the form with the subject and text for your message, then click to send it off. It'll then be displayed alongside all the other messages.

## //MAILING LISTS

Mailing lists are an efficient way of redistributing messages to a group of like-minded people. They are a great way to keep up to date with a special interest group or colleagues. Everything is done through your normal email program. When you want to post a message to the group, send it to the list's management email address; this then distributes your message to everyone else on the list. If anyone else posts a message to the list, you'll get it in your mailbox. Simple and effective.

Mailing lists were started by academics in the early days of the Internet, when email was the main tool. Now, mailing lists have proliferated to cover every imaginable area of discussion. There are over 90,000 specialist mailing lists that let you join and discuss everything from investment strategies to music.

Some mailing lists are moderated, which means the founder reads everything before it's relayed to the other members. If it's offensive or unsuitable, it will be deleted. Most mailing lists simply relay messages straight to the members.

Finding a mailing list is easy. Most of the search engines let you search the database of lists or, better still, visit one of the specialist mailing list sites such as Liszt (**www.liszt.com**). Search for a subject and you'll get a range of lists available. Most have mini descriptions and instructions on how to subscribe. For example, EuroUpdate provides an email discussion list for American companies that are interested in doing business in Europe. To join, visit the EuroUpdate site (**www.euroupdate.com**) and type in your email address in the online form.

### How to join

If the mailing list is open (most are), simply send an email message to the address of the automatic manager, called the List Server (usually written 'listserv'). In the main part of the message you'll need to type out a special instruction to tell the List Server that you want to subscribe to the list. The instruction tells the server that you want it to add your email address to the list. Once you've sent an email to the list server to join the list, you'll get any messages sent by other subscribers.

## //NEWSGROUPS

Newsgroups form one of the most active areas of the Internet – they provide an open forum that lets anyone discuss just about anything. There are tens of thousands of individual newsgroups, each providing a discussion forum for a particular subject. They work rather like a noticeboard – anyone can post a message that can then be read by any other user.

Unlike web-based discussion groups, which are stored on a single website, there's no single computer that stores all the newsgroups. Instead, the news servers at every Internet Service Provider swap information to ensure that they are all up to date. If you post a message, it'll appear instantly in the newsgroup stored on your ISP's news server, but it will take a few seconds (or minutes) before it is copied to all the other news servers in the area. Over the next few hours, your message will be automatically copied to all the news servers across the world.

To join in you'll need special software called a newsgroup reader – which lets you read notices and submit your own – and a normal connection to the Internet. Both Microsoft and Netscape include a newsgroup reader with their free email programs – there are alternative programs that you can download from the web, but the built-in readers are a good way to get started.

Newsgroups are divided into seven broad categories, called hierarchies, which differentiate the groups very roughly by type of subject. The main categories are:

- **comp** – computer-related newsgroups
- **misc** – groups that don't fit into the other categories
- **news** – discussions about the Usenet itself
- **rec** – hobbies and sports

- **sci** – science-orientated discussion
- **soc** – social issues
- **talk** – where anything goes.

In addition to the seven main categories, there is an eighth rogue category called 'alt', which contains a wide and wild range of newsgroups, some of which are controversial.

Each of the main hierarchies is divided into subcategories. For example, in the 'biz' hierarchy, there are the 'biz.jobs' and 'biz.marketplace' subcategories, which contain newsgroups about investment and jobs. Each level of organisation is separated by a full stop (or period); it makes it a little easier for you to have a good stab at guessing what a newsgroup is all about. For example, the 'biz.jobs.offered' newsgroup is devoted to discussion of job vacancies on offer.

### Finding a newsgroup

The first time you connect to your news server, your software will download the current list of newsgroups. You can browse through, looking for something that sounds interesting, or use your reader's filter function to narrow down the list to group titles that contain a particular word. However, until you visit the group, you'll never know quite how active, friendly or useful it really is.

---

A good way to find a newsgroup that's of interest is to use a specialist search engine, such as Remarq (www.remarq.com), Deja (www.deja.com) or Tile.Net (www.tile.net), to search through archives of newsgroup messages – you'll soon see which newsgroups are relevant. Alternatively, search for a newsgroup by its founder's description at http://alabanza.com/kabacoff/Inter-Links.

---

Newsgroup readers look and work in a very similar way to an email program: on the left there's usually a list of the newsgroups (or the selection that you have chosen as interesting) and on the right you'll see the title line of the latest postings. Click on the title and the full message is displayed.

Reading newsgroup messages when you're connected to the Internet is ideal but, depending on your ISP and the type of account you have, it could hike up your phone bill. The alternative is to download all the new messages from your selected newsgroups, then log off and read them offline. If you post any replies, wait till you've read all the messages, then dial up and send off your new messages.

---

So you don't make a complete idiot of yourself with your first posting, there are a couple of newsgroups dedicated to newcomers trying out the system: alt.test and misc.test are the main stamping grounds of newbies.

---

### Marketing to newsgroups and mailing lists

Almost all newsgroups and mailing lists have a no-business policy. If you barge in and post a message about your new wonder product, you'll be flamed (get hate mail) and will have achieved nothing. However, niche newsgroups and mailing lists often have subscribers who might be potential customers. Use the softly-softly approach to marketing – if someone asks a question or has a problem, answer it sensibly, without any plugs. Instead, make sure that your signature (the few lines at the bottom of each message) includes your company name and a link to your website. So long as you're contributing something useful to the group, you'll be safe. And as a result, some members might even visit your site to see what you do.

### Newsgroup identities

Every message posted to a newsgroup has the sender's email address. It's up to the sender to decide whether to supply a real or a fake email address. Most newsgroup users really don't want to be identified, so they provide a false email address.

In fact, this isn't the crime you might imagine, but a perfectly reasonable response to a major problem. Unscrupulous mailshot companies trawl through newsgroups picking up the email addresses and adding these to a mailing list that's then sold on. You can guarantee that, if you post a message under your real email address, you'll soon be bombarded with junk mail and spam.

When you configure your newsgroup reader, you need to enter an email address to identify your postings. If you have an Internet account with the option of several email addresses, you could use a spare address just for your newsgroup activity. Or, better still, sign up for a free email account such as Hotmail (**www.hotmail.com**) and use this instead.

### Ground rules

All three types of discussion forum let you say pretty much what you like (especially in a newsgroup) so long as it's related to the subject. But (and this is a big but) you must observe some basic etiquette when adding your own comments. Some of the rules are simply good manners; others are specified by the forum; but the majority are for your own protection. Here are some guidelines to follow:

1 When you post a message, never give out your home phone number or any other personal details.

2 Do not post any marketing message or product plug.

3 It's a wise precaution to use a dud or alternative email address for your postings.

4 Don't post the same message to a whole mass of forums (called spamming); this is particularly common in newsgroups and it annoys people in all the groups.

5 Make sure your postings are relevant to the group. If you're not sure, read the FAQ (Frequently Asked Questions)

for the group, which are sometimes posted as a message. The FAQ message will spell out the ground rules and acceptable subjects for discussion. If you can't find this FAQ message, visit **www.faqs.org** for a list of all the FAQs for all the newsgroups.

6   When you post a message, don't use CAPITALS – this is the online equivalent of shouting, and is considered very rude.

7   Use smileys when you're trying to be funny or sarcastic. Not everyone's got your highly developed sense of humour and they might need prompting. Just don't use more than a couple of smileys per message. :-)

8   Don't reply to a provocative or deliberately argumentative message (a flame), or you'll start a flame war (slanging match).

## //ADDRESS BOOK

### Mailing lists

*To find one of the 90,000 mailing lists that's just right for you, use one of the mailing list databases listed below. You can't search the material that's sent via a list but you can check the list's description, plus the vital instructions on how to subscribe (and leave). To get you started, here are some of the best lists around (if the list has no website address, use Liszt to get instructions about how to subscribe).*

| | |
|---|---|
| **CataList** | **www.lsoft.com/lists/listref.html** |
| **Liszt** | **www.liszt.com** |
| **Tile.net** | **www.tile.net** |

### Discussion groups and chat forums

*If you want to hear the latest gossip about a company, find a hot tip or just talk about your ideas for beating the stock market,*

*there's nowhere better than a discussion forum. These form part
of many websites and provide an area where visitors can read
previous messages, comment or add their own thoughts. In the
financial world you'll find a mix of new investors, experienced
brokers and hopeful speculators crowded in. To find a discussion
group, either check your favourite business website (it may well
have its own) or use a search engine such as Talkway
(www.talkway.com) or ForumOne (www.forumone.com).
Alternatively, try these well-known groups.*

**About.com**  http://entrepreneurs.about.com
A great guide to articles, sites and opinions covering business for
the brave-hearts and how to go-it-alone.

**Association for**  www.profunda.dk/
**International Business**  resources/business/aib.html
Talk shop with 9,000 members of this organisation (based in
Denmark) – a steady flow of messages makes its email discussion
group useful.

**Business Credit Talk**  www.igotit.com
Talk about credit terms and chasing bad debts.

**Business 2.0**  www.business2.com
The practical side of business in the post-Y2K era – essential reading
and discussions.

**BusinessWeek**  www.businessweek.com
Opinions of the readers of this international business magazine.

**Excite! Chat**  www.excite.com
Busy chat sessions for general gossip, but the small business rooms
are rather quiet.

**Fast Company**  www.fastcompany.com
Cool, trendy high-tech magazine and similar companies and their
wannabes congregate for occasionally supercilious conversations.

**Financial Times** www.ft.com
Discussion and comment – ususally intelligent, too – on the news stories in the paper.

**Fortune Magazine** www.fortune.com
Mag for high-fliers hosts three forums for personal finance, economics and corporate management.

**Guru.com** www.guru.com
Consultant or freelance professional? Chew the fat and pitch for work with similar souls.

**Harvard Business** www.hbsp.harvard.edu/
**School ListServs** listservs/
Didn't go to the college? Never mind, you can still join in their discussions.

**International Trade** www.intl-trade.com/wwwboard
What else but talk about international trade? The ideal place to read this is in an anonymous Moscow hotel with your sample case by your side, if the Internet link works.

**LinkExchange** www.linkexchange.com
Ideas and discussion about online advertising.

**mail-list.com** www.mail-list.com
Can't find what you want? Set up your own mailing list and discussion group.

**Nvst.com Funding Forum** www.nvst.com
Talk yourself silly about funding your next project.

**Optima Trade Board** www.trade-board.com
More noticeboard than discussion, you'll find business opportunities and job requests here.

**Publicity and Promotion** www.
**Discussion Board** free-publicity.com
Chat about ways to promote your website without spending a cent.

**Red Herring**                                    **www.redherring.com**
Chat that roughly follows the agenda of the snappy new-business
magazine covering the e-business revolution.

**Sage**                                    **www.sagesoft.co.uk/accounts/**
Where accountants go to talk about software, taxes, numbers –
and Sage software. You can meet a lot of Finance Directors here.

**SOHO Discussion Group**          **www.zdnet.com/cc/chat.html**
Tips and tricks for the (very) small business owner.

**Startup Network**     **www.delphi.com/startupnetwork/start/**
Discuss how best to raise your venture capital.

**Yahoo! Business**                      **http://messages.yahoo.com/**
**Finance**                         **yahoo/business_and_finance/**
If you're feeling talkative, you could get lost for days in here. One
of the best, with 8,000 forums about different ideas for business
success.

**Wired**                                              **www.wired.com**
Talk with like-minded trendy, rich, beautiful e-entrepreneurs.

**Women Entrepreneurs Online Network**     **www.weon.com**
The perfect place for women entrepreneurs to discuss business.

---

**E-zines**

---

*There are tens of thousands of brilliant, witty, irreverent,
influential, useful e-zines available. The hardest job is trying to
find where they are and how to subscribe. Almost all are delivered
by email on a daily, weekly or monthly basis (normally depending
on the editor's energy levels). There are very few places that try
to keep an index of the zines on the web; try these to find your
perfect match.*

**eZine Center**                            **www.ezinecenter.com**
**HotWired**                          **www.hotwired.com/zines/**
**eZine List**                                **www.list-city.com**

## Newsgroups

*The major search engines, including Excite!, Yahoo! and AltaVista, all now extend their reach to the Usenet but you can also use one of the specialist search engines below to help find material within each newsgroup, as well as the most suitable newsgroup for your interests. We've also listed some of the best-known and busiest financial newsgroups on the net.*

| | |
|---|---|
| **Deja** | **www.deja.com** |
| **Newsgroup Directory** | **http://Tile.net/news** |
| **Remarq** | **www.remarq.com** |
| **Usenet Info Center** | **http://metalab.unc.edu/usenet-i/** |

## Try these newsgroups

**alt.make.money.fast**
Wild schemes for instant riches.

**alt.biz.marketplace.international**
The chance to buy and sell around the world.

**alt.business**
Just about anything to do with business.

**alt.business.accountability**
Who's responsible for the mess?

**alt.business.career-opportunities.executives**
High flyers get top jobs.

**alt.business.franchise**
Set up a sandwich bar.

**alt.business.hospitality**
How to entertain clients.

**alt.business.import-export**
Tractors and cooking oil.

**alt.business.insurance**
Make sure you're covered.

**alt.business.internal-audit**
What to do when you get the call.

**alt.business.misc**
Off-the-wall – but sometimes actually about business.

**alt.business.multi-level**
How to make millions selling to friends.

**alt.business.multi-level.scam.scam.scam**
There be rogues out there.

**alt.business.seminars**
Listen to experts.

**biz.comp.accounting**
Crunching numbers on your computer.

**biz.entrepreneurs**
How to make it big, on your own.

**biz.marketplace**
Equipment for sale.

**clari.biz.briefs**
Today's business stories summarised.

**clari.biz.currencies**
What's up and down with the yen, dollar, pound …

**clari.biz.economy**
Reports and analysis on the (US) economy.

**clari.biz.industry**
Top company news and reports.

**misc.taxes**
US taxes. Yuck.

**misc.taxes.moderated**
US taxes without the abuse.

**sci.econ**
Gossip about the latest economic theories.

---

## Newsgroup reader software

*There's not much point switching from your web browser's integrated newsreader, unless you want a change of view. If you do, here are stand-alone programs that'll do the job.*

**Agent**                                    www.forteinc.com
All the gizmos you need but in a package that's hard to use. Costs $20 (about £14) to download the useful version, or get the freebie that does away with the best bits. PCs only.

**Gravity**                                  www.microplanet.com
Easy to use, with powerful filtering and support for reading messages offline, but costs $39.95 (about £26) – for PCs only.

**Hogwasher**                               www.asar.com
Decent newsreader and email program for Mac users – for $49.00 (around £32).

**Messenger**                               www.netscape.com
Reasonable everyday power wrapped in a friendly front end. Bundled with the Navigator web browser or you can download a PC or Mac version for free.

**News Rover**                              www.newsrover.com
Great for automating newsgroup message retrieval, but awkward to use and with a $29.95 (£20) price tag. For PCs only.

**NewsWatcher**                             www.filez.com
A classic newsgroup reader for the Macintosh available from any good shareware site. Developed at Northwest University (www. nwu.edu), it has masses of online support at educational sites.

**News Xpress**　　　　　　　　　　　　**www.download.com**

A free, basic reader that's easy for beginners to use, but not a patch on Outlook or Messenger. For PCs only.

**OutlookExpress**　　　　　　　　　　　**www.microsoft.com**

Bundled free with Internet Explorer or available for free download. For PC or Macs.

---

### Free email accounts

---

*Almost every portal and major site now offers visitors a free email address. These are a great way of separating work and personal or newsgroup messages. The drawback is that, usually, you can send and read messages only by using a clunky slow website. All of the following provide a similar service.*

| | |
|---|---|
| **Bigfoot** | **www.bigfoot.com** |
| **Cometmail** | **www.cometmail.com** |
| **Excite!** | **www.excite.com** |
| **Hotmail** | **www.hotmail.com** |
| **RocketMail** | **www.rocketmail.com** |
| **Yahoo!** | **www.yahoo.com** |

# 9//DIRECTORY

## //EVERY USEFUL SITE YOU NEED FOR YOUR BUSINESS

We've organised this directory into sections that cover just about every useful aspect of business on the Internet – from accountants to office supplies, from staff contracts to start-ups.

Although we've visited all the sites, the Internet never stops evolving and you may find that some of the names have changed as companies are bought, sold or merged. This is particularly relevant in the 'Business to Business' section: it's seeing astonishing growth and change. If you find a new site, or want to report a change of name you think is worth including in the next edition, please let us know by emailing us at response@virgin-pub.co.uk.

In most of the sections we've included a selection of Starting Points – sites that provide a general overview of the subject or that list a directory of sites on the topic. Use these if you're in a hurry and want a quick fix, but you'll find a lot more in-depth information in the specialist sites listed within the section. First of all, here's a select list of sites to get you started.

## //BUSINESS STARTING POINTS

One of the best places to start browsing for business information – regardless of what you're looking for – is within a business megasite or portal. In many other fields of the Internet, such as music, travel and money, portals have taken over as rulers of their domain and can cover everything related to the subject. It's not yet true of business sites – simply because of the diversity of information available. However, a few of these beasts have been developed and provide a useful one-stop briefing point, gathering together advice, information and news. We can expect to see many more business portals as the net community and business users realise the power of doing business through the Internet.

You'll find that some of these financial portals crop up within the rest of the directory – often because they provide the best sources of information for more than one subject. As you'll see from the rest of this directory, there are hundreds of specialist sites that often give better information about a particular product. But, for a quick answer, try one of these sites first.

**AllBusiness.com**                    **www.allbusiness.com**
Great place to sort out your major small-business worries, especially if you're in the USA. Get a loan, find new employees and check on bad debts or potential new customers.

**Bloomberg**                    **www.bloomberg.com**
Vast collection of news, market analysis and the latest prices – in five languages.

**British Chambers of Commerce**    **www.britishchambers.org.uk**
Central directory of the government-funded local chambers of commerce network that provide help and advice for any business.

**Confederation of British Industry (CBI)**        **www.cbi.org.uk**
Representation for all of British industry as a whole – lobbying government and international organisations.

**Dow-Jones**                    **www.businessdirectory.**
**Business Directory**                    **dowjones.com**
Great guide if you want lots of business news, features and comment – together with a fine directory of related sites.

**EOCenter**                    **www.eocenter.com**
Gathers together news and features from the major new business magazines and journals – for a concise report on what's happening to the future of business and technology.

**Federation of Small Businesses**        **www.fsb.org.uk**
So it's hardly a business megasite, but it's a nice way to start by finding an organisation championing the causes of small business

in the UK. For a more highbrow approach to a similar cause, visit the Institute of Directors (www.iod.co.uk)

**FinanceWise**                                   www.financewise.com
Impressive search engine designed solely to retrieve business and financial information from around the net.

**Inc. Online**                                         www.inc.com
Just about the best magazine site for entrepreneurs and enthusiastic business folk. Provides advice columns, discussion forums and a vast directory of online resources.

**Killerbiz**                                       www.killerbiz.com
Want to buy something for your business? Type in the spec for your insurance requirements, printing, telephone system, design service or payroll and you'll get a stack of quotes from eager merchants who want your business.

**Microsoft bCentral**                             www.bcentral.com
Microsoft gets just about everywhere – but as usual, this site is well designed, useful and full of advice for small-business people. Great, if you can ignore the plugs for Microsoft kit.

**Office.com**                                        www.office.com
One of the best business portals, with lots of advice, features and help topics, together with discussion groups, industry news and an e-commerce shop to fund it all.

**The Raging Bull**                              www.ragingbull.com
Want to see which bright spark beat you to the latest dot-com billion-dollar launch? Find out with the news, price data and the latest IPO (Initial Public Offering) forecasts.

**SmartAge**                                        www.smartage.com
There's a mass of features to help and advise small-business visitors on e-commerce – but it's all wrapped up in a pushy sales site selling business and office supplies.

**SmartOnline**                        www.smartonline.com
One-stop portal for small-business information. There are plenty of
software tools to download – though some will cost you – to help
incorporate your company, create a killer business plan, manage
your human resources or create a marketing scheme.

## //ACCOUNTS

Preparing your quarterly and year-end accounts will never rate as
one of the most enjoyable pastimes, but since most companies
(and their accountants) already use computer-based accounting
software, much of the drudgery has been reduced. Linking this
software to the Internet and automating the entire reporting
process is the next goal.

Software-based accounts programs, such as those from Intuit
(www.intuit.com) and Sage (www.sage.com), can manage basic
accounts, print cheques, sort out VAT, look after stock-control and
even do the payroll. And if you have the right combination of
accounts software and business bank account, you can link the
two together for an automatic transfer of information.

In the UK, the final piece of the accounts jigsaw has just been
produced by the Government: you can now file your tax forms over
the net. Of course, in the USA and Australia there's been a system in
place for ages that allows the net-savvy to fill in and submit their
tax returns from an official website. For example, US residents can
check the fabulous (and surprisingly witty) Internal Revenue Service
site (www.irs.gov) for news on paying tax online. And, to submit a
tax return, there are several independent sites; in many cases, your
personal-finance software – such as Intuit Quicken (www.quicken.
com) – provides a direct link to the IRS.

Regardless of how much computer power is thrown at the
accounting process, it's still a complex and, for many businesses,
time-consuming part of day-to-day management. It's essential for

analysis of sales, cashflow and projections, but needs skilled staff to set up and run the software. In most cases, your existing accountant should be able to help out. Most now have one computer expert on hand to advise their clients; some are beginning to offer two levels of service – one as a basic bureau checking computer-generated accounts to make sure you're using the software correctly, and the second providing full-service advisory and management accounting.

## Starting points

**Canada Customs and Revenue Agency (CCRA)**     **www.rc.gc.ca**
Canadians can make life a little easier by filing their tax returns via the web.

**Chartered Accountants**     **www.chartered-accountants.**
**Directory**     **co.uk**
OK, this may not be at the cutting edge of web design, and it'll never be one of those cult sites. But it does tell you where you can find your local qualified accountant in Britain.

**The Inland Revenue**     **www.inlandrevenue.gov.uk**
Plenty of clear instruction and information about how to manage and submit your accounts. And if you submit them online you'll get a discount off your tax bill.

**Internal Revenue**     **www.irs.ustreas.gov/**
**Service (IRS)**     **prod/bus_info/**
The US Government's good attempt to try to explain and clarify the mass of tax forms, regulations and allowances that you'll face when filing your business tax returns.

**Taxsites**     **www.taxsites.com**
Comprehensive directory of worldwide tax-based websites – the perfect place to find your local expert or regional tax office.

**UK Taxation Directory**     **www.uktax.demon.co.uk**
Tax software, publishers, specialists and trade organisations

are all listed in this simple, but useful, directory of British tax-related sites.

## Accountants

*To help choose a qualified accountant who is a specialist in your field, use one of the directories we've listed. All these list qualified accountants: in the UK this means the accountant's a member of a professional accounting body such as the ACCA (www.acca.co. uk); and in the US and Australia make sure you're dealing with a CPA (Certified Practising Accountant). Most of the directories let you search by area or speciality to find your perfect financial match.*

**ABIAF (Association of British Independent Accounting Firms)**     www.abiaf.co.uk
Small, select list of independent accountants who aim to make their subject jargon-free.

**ACCA (Association of Chartered Certified Accountants)**     www.acca.co.uk
Professional body for qualified accountants, with plenty of background material and advice on finding a suitable accountant.

**Accountant finder**     www.cpafinder.com
Find your dream accountant in the US by state or speciality.

**AccountantsDotCom**     www.accountantsdotcom.com
Claims to be the only site you'll need to visit, but at the moment it's just a directory of local accountants across the UK.

**Accountant-Search.com**     www.accountant-search.com
A searchable directory of over 100,000 American accountants organised by area and skill.

**Chartered Accountants Directory**     www.chartered-accountants.co.uk
Comprehensive directory of chartered accountants across the UK.

**Chartered Institute of Taxation**     www.tax.org.uk
Pay tax? Of course you do – but are you paying too much? Here's lots of useful information from the professionals.

**CPA Firms**     www.cpafirms.com
Search for an accountant in your area of the US.

**CPA Online**     www.cpaonline.com.au
Australians! Search out your nearest or best-qualified accountant. You could even search for both.

**CyberAccountant**     www.cyber-cpa.com
Helps you with tax questions or, if you're still stuck, you can find a local accountant.

**EuroAsPa**     www.euroaspa.com
Find an accountant anywhere in Europe, Asia or the Pacific (hence the acronym) in this modest, if wide-ranging, directory from consultants in north London.

**ICAEW (Institute of Chartered Accountants of England and Wales)**     www.icaew.co.uk
Guides and advice from one of the professional bodies governing accountants – with a well-hidden list of local companies.

**ICAS (Institute of Chartered Accountants of Scotland)**     www.icas.org.uk
Find a canny moneyman north of the border.

**Institute of Chartered Accountants In Australia**     www.icaa.org.au
Search for an accountant from the folk who set their exams.

**Krislyn's Favourite Accounting Sites**     http://sites.krislyn.com/acct.htm
Modest range of helpful, regulatory and informative sites about accounting – part of a great, larger, business-wide directory.

**PAYEcheck**                          www.payecheck.co.uk
Make sure that you've got your staff's tax and NI contributions
sorted out.

**Tax and Accounting Sites**            www.taxsites.com
Extensive directory of tax and accounting sites (centred mainly on
those in North America and Australia).

**Taxprofessionals.com**            www.taxprofessionals.com
IRS visiting? Find a professional to help.

**TriNET VCO**                          www.trinetvco.com
Don't waste time doing the payroll or managing your staff records,
outsource it to these folk.

### International accountants

*If you run a vast international conglomerate, you really ought to
speak to one of the vast international accountancy firms. They are:*

| | |
|---|---|
| **Arthur Andersen** | www.arthurandersen.com |
| **BDO Stoy Hayward** | www.bdo.co.uk |
| **Deloitte & Touche** | www.deloitte.co.uk |
| **Ernst and Young** | www.ernsty.co.uk |
| **Kidsons Impey** | www.kidsons.co.uk |
| **KPMG** | www.kpmg.com |
| **PriceWaterhouseCoopers** | www.pwcglobal.com |

### Accounting software

*Before you choose a new accounting software package, ask
your accountant which system they use and support – choose the
same and it'll make life so much easier when it's time to report
and audit. And if you plan to set up an online bank account,
check that the accounts software is supported by the bank; you
should be able to transfer your monthly account statement details
directly over the Internet into your accounts software – saving a
lot of typing.*

**Accounting Software Systems**            www.2020software.com

Evaluations and summaries of the leading accounting software on the market – so it's easier for you to choose.

**Accubooks 2000**            www.accubooks2000.com

Low-end budget accounting software for a small business.

**AccPac**            www.accpac.com

Accounting software for small- to medium-sized businesses – with lots of features to help tie in with your e-commerce site and manage sales, costs and profits.

**DacEasy**            www.daceasy.com

Without the graphical pretty face of Quicken or Money, DacEasy is still easy to use, and good for small businesses.

**Great Plains**            www.gps.com

A range of low-to-high-end accounting and reporting software that ties in tightly with standard Microsoft office software.

**Money**            www.microsoft.com/money/

Masses of features packed into this popular home and small-business finance-management software. It'll do everything from confirming your chequebook balance to paying bills online via your Internet bank (see page 156).

**MYOB**            www.myob.com

Manage your cash flow, stock control and payroll with this accounting software aimed at companies with a turnover below £1m. It walks the fine line between stacks of features and ease of use – and, unusually, it works on PCs and Macs.

**Peachtree Accounting**            www.peachtree.com

Accounting software that keeps winning awards for features and ease of use. The product range covers software to help a one-man band operation right up to medium-sized businesses with dozens of order clerks.

**QuickBooks**                      www.quickbooks.com
Just about the best-known range of accounting software that
revolutionised the way these products look and work. Developers
Intuit were the first to make the screen layout look like the paper
equivalent (of a cheque or ledger book). Simple to use, powerful
and well supported, there's also Quicken (www.quicken.com) for
self-employed and personal finance applications.

**QuickTax**                        www.quicktax.co.uk
Check your tax return and make the most of all your allowances. In
the US, the equivalent product is called TurboTax (www.
turbotax.com).

**ResourcePhoenix**                 www.resourcephoenix.com
Fed up installing special computer hardware and software to run
your accounts software? Let someone else do it – outsource it to
these specialists. You pay a monthly fee and they provide exactly
what you want, via simple Internet links, to software running on
their central computers.

**Sage**                            www.sage.co.uk
The leading accounting software for small- to medium-size
businesses is supported by just about every accountant in the UK
and provides a safe, sensible route to computerising and managing
your accounts.

**TaxCalc**                         www.idp.co.uk
Software from Which? magazine to help the self-employed fill in
tax forms – and make the most of your allowances.

**TaxSaver**                        www.microsoft.com
Leads you step by step through the business of analysing your
accounts, then suggests ways to save tax before finally completing
your return.

# //ADVICE AND GUIDES

A business owner has a lot to worry about. There's staff, cashflow, marketing, sales, accounts, paperclips. And if you're starting a business, there are problems and obstacles everywhere. Even the most proficient business polyglots will only be expert in a few of these areas. What you need is advice.

You could turn to a professional consultant who'll be able to look at your business plan, accounts, marketing or sales and suggest ways to improve things. But, if you have the time and energy, you can use the Internet to do that work for you. It's packed with guides, reports, forecasts and charts that'll tell you as much as, if not more than, the average adviser. And, best of all, most of it's free. Visit a couple of sites and you'll pick up great advice from some of the best-known business gurus.

Some business advice is aimed at those starting their first company. If this is you then you probably know all about the industry you're entering, but have you ever had to draw up a business plan, deal with staff and tax paperwork or manage cashflow? And if you're already running a business, there are usually enough new challenges to make advice essential; it's usually for the one-off and unusual jobs that you'll need help. How do you set up a staff pension, expand the company, move into new markets or simply re-work your marketing strategy? There are plenty of great guides for anyone new to business explaining first principles; but there are also guides to help business people with management and strategy problems.

## Starting points

**American Management Association**  **www.amanet.org**
A good directory of seminars, courses, self-study material and features that'll help you understand management principles and practice.

**Business Associations**                    www.ibf.com/ba/ibba.htm
Your local business centre is one of the best sources of information, advice and guides. This directory lists thousands around the world.

**Business Link**                            www.businesslink.co.uk
Government-funded network of advice centres around the UK that help local businesses with information, advice and expertise on just about every aspect of business. Find your local centre on this site.

**EntreWorld**                               www.entreworld.org
A rare gem – a content-only site provided by a charity that helps improve entrepreneurship and business skills. Masses of concise features pulled from other commercial and academic sites covering how to start, manage and make the most of your business.

---

**Business advice**

---

**AllBusiness.com**                          www.allbusiness.com
Masses of advice, forms, services and business content and resources to browse. But you're never allowed to forget this is an e-commerce site.

**American Express**                         www.americanexpress.com
**Small Business Exchange**                              smallbusiness
Wondering if your company's too small to outsource? Or maybe you just want advice on loans? AmEx provides this very useful resource centre – but it's geared to US business people, and over-loaded with ads for their credit cards.

**Business Resource Center**                 www.morebusiness.com
Heaps of articles and advice on starting, running and managing your business.

**CommerceNet**                              www.commerce.net
A gang of high-tech companies that do business over the net – find out how they work and what's happening in development.

**Enterprise Zone**       www.enterprisezone.org.uk
Good source of business, financial, marketing, legal, training and export news and advice geared towards British companies.

**EnterWeb**       www.enterweb.org
Great directory of links and articles that'll help you find any type of information – from finance deals to help with starting or managing a small business.

**Entrepreneurial Edge Online**       www.edgeonline.com
Practical advice on running and developing your business. Some of the sample letters are off the mark for the UK, but the financial toolbox alone is worth the visit.

**Fast Company**       www.fastcompany.com
The first and foremost of a new breed of business magazines aimed at hi-tech companies and entrepreneurs. The printed version is great; the online version is better – it's free.

**Garage.com**       www.garage.com
Apple and Hewlett-Packard were founded in a garage; here's a virtual version packed with help for anyone starting a high-tech business.

**Inc. Online**       www.inc.com
Just about the best magazine site for entrepreneurs and enthusiastic business folk. Provides advice columns, discussion forums and a vast directory of online resources.

**Microsoft bCentral**       www.bcentral.com
Microsoft gets just about everywhere – but as usual, this site is well designed, useful and full of advice for small-business people – if you can ignore the plugs for Microsoft kit.

**Office.com**       www.office.com
One of the best business portals, with lots of advice, features and help topics together with discussion groups, industry news and an e-commerce shop to fund it all.

**SmartOnline**                           **www.smartonline.com**
One-stop portal for small-business information. There are plenty of
software tools to download – though some will cost you – to help
incorporate your company, create a killer business plan, manage
your human resources or create a marketing scheme.

**GovWorks**                              **www.govworks.com**
Direct access to the US local government departments – ask
questions, check regulations or pay your bills; a model of the future
open government strategies. If you want to do business with the
US government, head to GovCon (**www.govcon.com**) for information about current contract tenders.

**Guru**                                  **www.guru.com**
Snappy, charged meeting place for consultants, freelancers or
anyone who calls their kitchen their office. Packed with advice,
jobs, trendy gizmos and financial help.

**Online Women's Business Center**        **www.onlinewbc.org**
Stacks of advice, information, discussion and tutorials geared to
women running companies.

**Wilson Internet Services**              **www.wilsonweb.com**
Yes, Ralph's a consultant, but the site is a gem. It includes his well-
written newsletters on just about every aspect of Internet
commerce and marketing. If you're planning a business website or
an update, visit and read good advice.

---

**Management and management gurus**

---

**Alliance of Consultants**        **www.allianceofconsultants.com**
Not sure how to manage something yourself? Find a consultant to
help with your new project, or just help run the business more
effectively. The core database has consultants located around the
world who can help with everything from management to design.

**American Management Association**        **www.amanet.org**
One of the biggest management organisations around, working as

a (gentle) lobbying group, but mainly helping business people discuss and improve their management skills through seminars, training courses and books.

**Edwards Deming: his teachings**  www.deming.org
Renowned for his Total Quality concepts, here are the thoughts of Deming and their application. Or try a condensed version in Deming's 14 Points (http://deming.ces.clemson.edu)

**Peter F. Drucker**  www.drucker.org
Unusually, compared to his peers, management guru Drucker has set up a non-profit site that contains some of his articles, many of his ideas and a lot of practical advice and reports. An essential stop for anyone in management.

**Electronic Intelligence**  www.anbar.co.uk/
**Management Library**  management
Want to read a management article? This site acts as a library to tens of thousand of them, originally published in journals and business magazines – often written by top management experts. Read and learn.

**The Glass Ceiling**  www.theglassceiling.com
Why haven't I been offered that top management job? The old theories (and lobbying tack of this group) suggested that companies were reluctant to offer women top jobs. Now, the position's changed slightly and this site covers the trials and tribulations facing women and ethnic or minority interest groups who feel that they are as well qualified as their colleagues but are always ignored for promotion.

**Charles Handy:**  www.drucker.org/leaderbooks/
**The Search for Meaning**  L2L/summer97/handy.html
It's hard getting the words of wisdom of guru Charles Handy for free, but this interesting article gives an overview of his thoughts and principles – and has links to related management sites.

**Harvard Business School Publishing**   www.hbsp.harvard.edu
Management guru John P. Kotter teaches at the famous school; read his and other reports and briefings on management techniques and styles.

**Leadership Communications**   www.lc21.com
**for the 21st Century**
Practical hints, tips and advice to help managers improve their leadership skills and manage effectively – or even how to write a good speech to stir up the troops or shareholders.

**Management General**   www.mgeneral.com
Webzine for anyone in management who wants to improve their skills or learn what guru Tom Brown has to say on the matter of leadership.

**Selection of Management**   www.rushmans.com/imc/
**Consultants**   page6.html
It's hardly surprising that the Institute of Management Consultants packs its site with reports and encouragement on hiring a consultant. This particular document provides a good overview of what you have to do and pay, and what you should expect in return.

**TrainingSuperSite**   www.trainingsupersite.com
Mammoth collection of training, research and support documents to help HR departments work with and improve the skills of the management (and other sectors) within their company.

**Women's Institute of Management**   www.jaring.my/wimnet
A good place for women to discuss ideas and find information to help them improve their leadership skills, training and promotion prospects in their company.

**International management consultants**

*If you're experiencing rapid growth with turnover in the millions, want help with accounting across your group, plan to revolutionise your basic business model or simply want outside* expert advice on strategy then you might find management consultants useful. There are small, specialist companies, such as Zefer (*www.zefer.com*) and Zland (*www.zland.com*), which can help you work out an effective e-strategy. Alternatively, use one of the big international companies; they can handle any business project but are well known for their high hourly charges. To find out what's on offer, here are some of the biggest international companies. Don't expect answers from their websites – all will want to meet and discuss the task and the terms before taking on a job.

| | |
|---|---|
| **Andersen Consulting** | **www.ac.com** |
| **Bain & Company** | **www.bain.com** |
| **Booz-Allen & Hamilton** | **www.bah.com** |
| **Deloitte Consulting** | **www.dc.com** |
| **Ernst & Young** | **www.ey.com** |
| **KPMG** | **www.kpmg.com** |
| **McKinsey & Co.** | **www.mckinsey.com** |
| **Mercer Management Consulting** | **www.mercermc.com** |

## Starting a business

**BT Partnership**  www.partnership.bt.com
Dominant UK telco dishes out news and advice for global (read Internet) business methods.

**Corporate**  www.corporate.com
From Delaware to Texas, if you want to incorporate in any US state you can do it in a click from here.

**Small Business Administration**  www.sba.gov
The US Government's often annoyingly simplistic information source. Helps you put together a business plan and start up your dream.

**StartUps.com**  www.startups.com
Got a great idea, but don't know where to go next? This company

provides everything for a new company, from loan sources to furniture – for a fee.

**Your Business –**          **www.microsoft.com/uk/**
**Microsoft UK**          **yourbusiness/**

Techie advice from the Seattle HQ to help small business owners make the most of IT.

### Business plans

*A well-conceived business idea needs a good business plan.*
*It details your strategy, business model and targets for sales,*
*turnover, profits and overheads. When you open your business*
*bank account or ask for a loan, you'll need to produce a good*
*business plan. It's not too hard to come up with a plan using a*
*word processor, but if you want help to make sure you tackle*
*every point, try these templates and software:*

**Bplans.com**          **www.bplans.com**
**Business Resource Software**     **www.businessplans.org**
**BusinessTown.com**     **www.businesstown.com/planning**
**BizPlanIt**          **www.bizplanit.com/vplan.htm**

### Buying or selling a business

**BizBuySell**          **www.bizbuysell.com**

Just about the biggest database of businesses and franchise opportunities for sale – over 10,000 to choose from. And before you sign up for that chicken farm in Utah, there's plenty of advice, support groups and sample paperwork to help you make the right business choice.

**Business For You**          **www.business4u.com**

Hundreds of companies – generally smaller, entrepreneur-style opportunities – on offer across the US (with the odd international one thrown in for good measure). No way as slick or sophisticated a presentation as BizBuySell.

**Businesses for Sale**          www.businessforsale.com

As you'd guess from the title, it's a general database of businesses and franchises for sale around the world. Not as sleek as BizBuySell but with a wider range on offer than Business for You.

**Daltons**          www.daltons.co.uk

Buy a pub or get a franchise from the weekly classified magazine listing business opportunities, premises, franchises and other deals.

**Exchange and Mart**          www.exchangeandmart.co.uk

Business classifieds – from business equipment to businesses.

**Moore, Wood**          www.mwclicproperty.
**& Cockram**          demon.co.uk

Buy a pub or restaurant from this specialist company that deals in nothing else.

---

### Franchises

---

*If you are eager to set up on your own, but you still want the help and backing of a large company, you might find operating a franchise is a good solution. You pay a fee to use the brand name, signs and logo of a well-known chain and usually pay a percentage of the takings back to the original company. Most of the chains of high-street sandwich bars, restaurants, service stations and print-shops are run in this way; the shop is owned (or leased) and run by an individual, who buys instant recognition and a stack of marketing and business advice from the parent company. There are hundreds of franchise opportunities available – but you should look carefully at the history of the company and what's on offer for your investment. These sites offer advice and directories of franchises available in your area.*

**American Association of Franchisees & Dealers**    www.aafd.org

Want a franchise? Think your company can be franchised? Plenty of advice for both sides, as well as help if it all goes wrong.

**The Australia Franchise Council**　　　www.fca.com.au
Regulations and advice from the official organisation covering franchise opportunities in Australia.

**Be the Boss**　　　www.betheboss.com
How to set up on your own, with a franchise. Lots of tips for newcomers, links to potential operators and general business advice to keep you going.

**The British Franchise Association**　　www.british-franchise.org.uk
Don't get ripped off; check the list of accredited advisors and franchise suppliers before signing up. To get you up and running, there's plenty of advice and, to pay for it all, seminars and books.

**Canadian Business Franchise Magazine**　　　www.cgb.ca
How to go about getting and running a franchise in Canada.

**Centercourt**　　　www.centercourt.com
Advice for aspiring entrepreneurs – an impressive range of business advice and franchise opportunities in North and South America and the UK.

**Federal Trade Commission –**　　　www.ftc.gov/
**Franchises**　　　bcp/franchise/
The official US government line on franchises with advice on how to avoid problems.

**FranchiseNet**　　　www.franchise.net.au
Setting up down-under? Lots of advice, regulations, business tips and franchise opportunities in Australia.

**The Franchise Registry**　　　www.franchiseregistry.com
A list of franchise opportunities in the US that have been approved for small business loans by a network of banks.

**FranInfo**　　　www.franinfo.co.uk
More advice and UK franchise opportunities than you could know what to do with.

**Franchising and franchises**  www.franchisedirect.co.uk
Masses of clear advice and guides to help you choose and run a franchise.

**Planet Smoothie**  www.planetsmoothie.com
Set up your frozen yoghurt drink concession. Well, lots of people like this stuff.

**Subway**  www.subway.com
Fed up buying your sandwiches from the local deli? Get a slice of the action and start your own sandwich shop.

## Stress management

*Most small-business people live on coffee and stress. It might make for a charged atmosphere and zingy, twitchy personality, but it's not terribly healthy. And if your employees are over-stressed, you'll end up losing time when they are ill at home – or suing you for not protecting their health. Try these sites to minimise and manage stress:*

| | |
|---|---|
| **American Institute of Stress** | www.stress.org |
| **Stress Management** | www.suite101.com |
| **Stress Stop** | www.stressstop.com |
| **Wes Sime Stress Management** | www.unl.edu/stress/ |

## SOHO (Small Office/Home Office)

**Business Matters**  www.business.knowledge.com
Friendly site that offers basic advice – from bookkeeping to marketing – on getting a business idea off the ground.

**Home-based Business**  www.smartbiz.com/sbs/cats/home.htm
Jumbled mass of features about working from home or starting a business at home. Useful, but hardly the peak of elegant design.

**Home Office Association of America**  www.hoaa.com
Americans take their SOHO concepts seriously – ideas, benefits,

advice and case studies from the official promoter of home-based workers.

**Small and Home Based Business Links**          www.bizoffice.com
You might not have big-company worries, but there's still plenty of bother with finance, marketing, news, opportunities and management. This directory is heaped full of links and advice geared to smaller businesses.

**Small Business 2000**          **www.sb2000.com**
Great collection of articles and TV features that tell potential entrepreneurs how to create, build and grow their little companies.

**The Small Business Advisor**          **www.isquare.com**
Stressed out, or just wondering how to market your gizmo? Whatever the small-business problem, there's probably a feature about it here.

**Smart Business Super Site**          **www.smartbiz.com**
Design-less site with assorted collections of links, advice, features, news and other stuff that's useful for any small business.

**Yahoo! Small**   http://uk.dir.yahoo.com/Business_and_Economy/
**Business Information**          Small_Business_Information/
The big Y's directory of useful sites for smaller British businesses.

---

**Legal advice**

---

*If you are having a dispute with an employee or a distributor, want to chase debts from a customer or simply want to finalise a contract for new offices, you could need a lawyer. Use an online database to find a suitable match that works nearby and specialises in your industry. If you want to hire a lawyer in another country, either try the international directories of law firms or contact the local British Council office (www.britcoun.org) in that country, which might be able to recommend a company.*

**ABA Network Lawyer Locator** www.abanet.org/martindale.html
How many lawyers do you need to make a website? This vast
database lists over 900,000 members of the American Bar
Association practising in the US; search for your perfect match.

**Attorney Net** **www.attorneynet.com**
Find an attorney who's local – in your US state – and who offers the
specialist knowledge you need.

**CaseMatch** **www.casematch.com**
Type in your legal problem – from property conveyancing to
bankruptcy – and this database will find a local US lawyer who can
handle the case.

**CataLaw Legal Directories** **www.catalaw.com**
A directory of directories – probably the best place to start looking
for a lawyer in the US, UK, Australia or Canada.

**World Law Guide** **www.lexadin.nl/wlg/**
Got a problem with an export customer? Find a lawyer in another
country – over 5,000 firms listed.

---

**Patents and trademarks**

*Now you've created your new invention, it's time to come up with
a name – and make sure that no one else has had the same idea.
Use the online patent and trademark databases to check that your
intellectual property is not being used by someone else – and that
you're not inadvertently using another's trademark.*

**All about Trademarks** **www.ggmark.com**
As you'd guess from the title, you'll find information about
registering and using trademarks, links to advisers and government
agencies, together with legal specialists.

**American Intellectual Property Law Association** **www.aipla.org**
Rather dry and austere, but official view on the use and misuse of
patents.

**Corporate Intelligence**                    **www.1790.com**
Research service that'll check millions of patents and trademarks to help you avoid infringing someone else's property.

**European Patent Office**                    **www.epo.co.at/epo/**
Based in Vienna, the EPO monitors patent registrations around Europe.

**IBM Patent Server**                         **www.patents.ibm.com**
Don't pay for patent research – instead, search IBM's database of a couple of million patents online. You only have to pay if you want a copy mailed to you.

**INTA**                                      **www.inta.org**
Worried about trademarks? This charity helps to promote effective policy on trademarks and patents; for surfers, it's dry and dusty, but there's background information hidden away inside.

**KuesterLaw**                                **www.kuesterlaw.com**
Directory of links covering intellectual property law – kindly provided by the eponymous law firm.

**Trademark Database**               **www.uspto.gov/tmdb/index.html**
Search the official US Government's database of trademarks – for free. If you find a clash or problem with your own words, you should go to a specialist lawyer.

**Patent Cafe**                               **www.patentcafe.com**
If you've just devised a fabulous widget, the guides here will help you to ensure it's protected by patents. Heaving with guides, links, advice, databases and tips to help everyone understand and use patents and trademarks correctly.

**The Patent Office**                         **www.patent.gov.uk**
An essential first stop for anyone concerned about patents. The British Government's office provides limited advice but plenty of news and official forms. You can request a patent or trademark search, but it takes several days and will cost you. Maybe they

should look to the US Government's site (**www.uspto.gov**) that's free and instant.

**Patents**                                                **www.uspto.gov**
The US Government's clear and friendly explanations on the way patents and trademarks work, how to patent an invention and what to do if your patent's been breached. And you can search the Government's database of patents here, too.

## //BUSINESS TO BUSINESS

Buy anything for your company cheaply and efficiently – that's the promise of the massive interest in business-to-business (often written B2B) websites such as Mondus (**www.mondus.com**) or KillerBiz (**www.killerbiz.com**). In this section, we've covered all the major items you'll need for your business – from the big and expensive, such as a van or new office – to the tiny and mundane, such as paperclips and pens.

You'll probably visit the office equipment sites most often, but for a big contract or new supplier, try one of the central procurement websites. Type in what you want – from marketing advice to office furniture – and it'll be routed to a group of tied suppliers who then bid, anonymously, for the work. The central site takes a slice of the action, and often charges the tied suppliers for the privilege of being part of the network.

Other sites act as business auction houses, giving you the chance to buy or sell used or surplus equipment and stock. If you need new filing cabinets, a supply of oil pumps or think you can turn a profit on surplus shirts, place your bid. Each item is normally part of the auction for a few days, so you can always up your bid as the closing deadline nears.

And lastly, there are plain online shops. The majority of online shops are still consumer-oriented, but some companies, notably office equipment suppliers, are moving online. These are often set up by existing catalogue companies, such as Viking (**www.viking.co.uk**) or Staples (**www.staples.com**). For more information, and hundreds of online shops, try the companion book *The Virgin Internet Shopping Guide*.

So far, very few small, niche business-to-business or material suppliers actually trade online, though this is sure to change soon. This means that if you're after a ton of grommets or a case of light bulbs you'll need to phone the wholesaler direct – or put in a bid request with a central procurement website.

---

### Starting points

**BizBuyer**                                   **www.bizbuyer.com**
Buy stuff for your company – from insurance to legal services, office equipment to computers. Geared to the US market, it's a model that's sure to spread.

**Exchange and Mart**               **www.exchangeandmart.co.uk**
Weekly newspaper that's packed with small ads offering office stuff for sale – the online version is updated in real time, and it's free.

**Killerbiz**                                   **www.killerbiz.com**
Want to buy something for your business? Type in the spec for your insurance requirements, printing, telephone system, design service or payroll and you'll get a stack of quotes from eager merchants who want your business.

**Mondus**                                      **www.mondus.com**
Whatever you want – a laptop, chair, marketing advice, courier, printing services and so on – submit a request for a quote and wait for the tied companies to supply bids.

**OrderZone**                                   **www.orderzone.com**
If your shopping list includes computer supplies, oil pumps,

semiconductors, or any stuff, this site lets you buy them all online, get one invoice and save money, time and effort.

**B2BNow**                                    **www.b2bnow.com**
A vast mall of online business suppliers – over half a million of them – are waiting to provide just about anything you might want.

## Specialist business to business

**Buzzsaw**                                    **www.buzzsaw.com**
Complete portal to help manage projects, create specs, bid for materials or just provide news.

**CheMatch.com**                              **www.chematch.com**
Trade chemicals, plastics and fuel products with others in the chemical industry.

**Grainger**                                   **www.grainger.com**
Power tools, grommets and stuff to fix other things for sale from this bright, breezy catalogue.

**Standard & Poors Platt's**                  **www.platts.com**
Trade petrol and oil products – a slick site that's packed with news and prices.

## Surplus and second-user goods

**BizSurplus**                                **www.bizsurplus.com**
Buy or sell just about any industrial equipment online.

**DoveBid**                                    **www.dovebid.com**
Astonishingly sophisticated online business auction site. Either bid online or watch the live video auctions in action – with over half a million items on offer, covering everything from complex test equipment to office chairs.

**iMARK.com**                                  **www.imark.com**
Gathers together thousands of sources of used industrial equipment to provide a one-stop hunting ground for buyers.

### OpenSite                                    www.opensite.com
Bidding room where buyers and sellers meet to haggle over equipment.

### SupplierMarket.com                     www.suppliermarket.com
Meeting place where buyers and sellers of parts and services can bid for work. If you want a particular widget for production, type in a request and wait for the bids to roll in – then choose the one you want.

### SurplusBin                               www.surplusbin.com
If you've got a warehouse full of unwanted goods, use this online auction site to sell them off to someone keen to fill their empty warehouse. As with personal auction sites, you pay a percentage to sell your goods, but it's a simple and effective way of buying or selling surplus stock and equipment – and one that's gaining ground as a legitimate alternative to using specialist brokers. You'll find a similar service, with similar activity, on TradeOut (www. tradeout.com).

### Worth Guide                              www.worthguide.com
Wondering how much your surplus stock is worth? Check past surplus auction results for an instant quote.

---

## Office equipment

---

### Ashfields                                www.ashfields.com
Furnish your office or reception with a good range of desks, chairs and sofas.

### Better Buys for Business                www.betterbuys.com
Concise guides that help you choose the best type of fax, copier or printer.

### Buyers Zone                              www.buysmart.com
Visit for the copious reviews and guides to help you buy office stuff – and an online shopping cart if you're in the US and want to buy it from here.

**Center for Office Technology**  www.cot.org
Hold it – are you sure that chair's ergonomically sound? This organisation provides good advice to improve the office environment.

**Exchange and Mart**  www.exchangeandmart.co.uk
Business classifieds – the ads have everything you'll need to fill an office.

**Harmen Miller**  www.harmenmiller.com
Just about the coolest, trendiest, most comfortable office chairs on the market. I want one.

**Neat Ideas**  www.neat-ideas.com
Online office stationery and equipment catalogue.

**Office Depot**  www.officedepot.com
Vast range of office equipment for sale in the US.

**Office Products**  www.officeproducts.com
Office equipment for sale, but wrapped in a bright and breezy site that's full of good advice, reviews and tips.

**The Office Shop**  www.owa.co.uk
Staplers to printers, paper pads to PCs – at low prices.

**Small Office**  www.smalloffice.com
Plenty of earnest discussion about office things for smaller companies – but with useful guides and reviews of equipment you'll need.

**Staples**  www.staples.com
Huge discount office supplier – the online shop bursting with everything from chairs to, er, staples. In the UK, you'll have to be content for the moment with a directory of local shops.

**Turnstone Furniture**  www.turnstonefurniture.com
Want a smart-looking office? Here's a good place to start looking for chairs and tables.

**Viking Direct**                    **www.viking-direct.co.uk**
The office bible now online; its catalogue of stationery, office
equipment, pens and paperclips is hard to beat, but rival Neat Ideas
comes close with a similar range and pricing.

## Stationery

**Business Stationery Direct**            **www.bsdstat.co.uk**
Use an accounting program to print your cheques and invoices?
This supplier's dedicated to selling the standard, pre-printed forms
and cheques you'll need.

**Buy.co.uk**                         **www.buy.co.uk**
An ambitious bulk-buying system that aims to cut the prices of just
about everything, from stationery to cars, mobile phones to travel.
And it works.

**EcoIreland**                       **www.ecoireland.com**
More companies should use environmentally friendly products –
and stationery's a good place to start. This site provides plenty
of alternative options to the usual planet-harming stuff we use
every day.

**Kall-Kwik Printing (UK) Ltd**          **www.kallkwik.co.uk**
The high-street franchised printer hits the web. Although it
promises much, it's still more a catalogue and doesn't yet let you
order or book a print run without visiting your local shop. Deadly
rival Prontaprint (**www.prontaprint.co.uk**) has a similarly dull
catalogue website.

**Multiquotes**                      **www.multiquotes.co.uk**
Before you write out a print purchase order for your new catalogue
or flyer, send this site an email with your requirements. You'll get
quotes from a dozen printers by return.

**Stamps Direct**                    **www.rubber-stamps.co.uk**
Not postage, but rubber – painless online ordering so you'll soon

be stamping papers with 'urgent', 'confidential' or whatever else you want to say.

**Stat Plus**                                      **www.statplus.co.uk**
Issue a writ – a vast range of legal forms and specialist legal stationery you might need.

**The Green Stationery Company**              **www.greenstat.co.uk**
No, it's not green-coloured envelopes and paper, but environmental stationery supplies – to help make your office less harmful to the environment.

---

## Postage

---

*Electronic mail poses a huge threat to the traditional postal service, but snail mail is fighting back. The argument seems to be that email is threatening the fax rather than the letter – if you need to send a contract or a catalogue, you still need to post an original document. The main postal services use their sites to reinforce this point with impassioned arguments of the benefits of direct mail. The Internet has, however, brought two new areas of business to postal services. The first is delivering goods you order from a website – rivalling the service offered by courier companies; the second is the development of electronic stamps. These provide a secure way to buy and print legal stamps on to your envelopes. If you haven't installed a franking machine, it's a lot simpler than licking and sticking old-fashioned paper stamps.*

**e-stamp.com**                                    **www.estamp.com**
Like stamps.com (below), these guys give you the chance to buy and print stamps from your desktop. There's normally a 10% premium on the cost of the postage and, thanks to the rivalry between these two companies, there are often great deals – like $50 (about £33) of free postage – on offer.

**Pitney Bowes**                              **www.pitneybowes.com**
Just about every office has a franking machine – and these folk have the main market share.

## Royal Mail                                    www.royalmail.co.uk

Impressive and highly credible argument by the UK's traditional postal service as to why you should stick with paper and stamps rather than switch entirely to email and website marketing. Yes, it's more expensive to use the post, but most consumers still seem to prefer to read a letter or handle a paper catalogue. And, tucked away on the site, you'll also find tools to search for postcodes or calculate postal rates.

## Stamps.com                                         www.stamps.com

Buy postage credits, then use the special software to (legally) print US stamps directly from your computer. Great for SOHOs that don't want a franking machine.

## United States Postal Service (USPS)            www.usps.com

Stacks of advice to help you with direct postal marketing and plenty of reasons why you should stick with the postal service rather than email and courier companies for marketing and fulfilment. Even with this agenda, they still add in bill payment, a zip code database and a way to buy old-fashioned sticky stamps online.

## Courier companies

*If you need to send something in a hurry, you'll need something that's quicker than a first-class or airmail postal service. There are several international courier companies that offer worldwide delivery in one or two days. Rates and delivery time depends on where your office is located. Almost all now have online tracking, so you can check via the net that your parcel's arrived.*

| | |
|---|---|
| **City Link** | www.city-link.co.uk |
| DHL | www.dhl.co.uk |
| **Federal Express** | www.fedex.com |
| **Parcel Force** | www.parcelforce.co.uk |
| **Securicor-Omega** | www.securicor.co.uk |
| TNT | www.tnt.co.uk |
| UPS | www.ups.com |

# Telephones

*Every business needs a telephone; use the net to find the cheapest supplier for the installation, phone line rental and the equipment itself. Whether you want a new mobile phone or a new hard-wired office telephone exchange, there are suppliers ready with discounts and offers online.*

**BT Shop**                                    **www.btshop.bt.com**

Connect with BT and shop from their range of phones, faxes and pagers. There's good advice on choosing the right equipment and a reasonable choice of models, but you'll find lower prices in specialist shops.

**buy.co.uk**                                    **www.buy.co.uk**

Find the cheapest source for your mobile phone bill and save money.

**Call2.com**                                    **www.call2.com**

Clever technology that lets you add a button to your websites – when a visitor clicks it, you're alerted and asked to phone the potential customer.

**Cambridge ISDN**                            **www.cambridge-isdn.com**

Kit out your office with the latest ISDN-based digital telephone exchange and computer network – you can surf at high speed as you answer calls.

**Carphone Warehouse**                    **www.carphonewarehouse.com**

Mobile phones, pagers and accessories from the giant chain.

**Cellnet**                                    **www.cellnet.co.uk**

Sign up and buy a phone online.

**Cheaper Calls UK**                        **http://cheapercalls.8m.com**

Cut the cost of your Orange or One2One mobile phone bills with the help of this provider.

**Future Numbers**                            **www.future-numbers.co.uk**

Don't just stick to the boring phone number you've been allocated, rent a memorable number that spells something or sounds good on a radio advert.

**Miah Telecom**  www.miah-telecom.co.uk
Subscribe to any of the pre-pay or standard mobile tariffs from the major networks, with a good range of handsets.

**Mobile Bargains**  www.mobilebargains.com
Good choice of pre-pay mobiles and top-up cards, accessories, car-kits and pagers.

**One2One**  www.one2one.co.uk
Buy a new mobile online.

**Orange**  www.orange.co.uk
Basic marketing and messaging services explained.

**Sagem Online**  www.sagem-online.com
Fax machine melted? Get a new one from this specialist supplier of faxes and phones for business customers.

**TalkingShop**  www.talkingshop.co.uk
Cheap mobile phones, with regular special offers.

**Virgin Mobile**  www.virgin.com/mobile/
Our very own mobile phone company.

**Vodafone**  www.vodafone-retail.co.uk
Subscribe and buy mobiles and accessories.

**Telephone over the Internet**
_____

*With a little extra (normally free) software, a set of speakers and a microphone, you can make long-distance phone calls over the Internet. And, with just a little extra hardware, you can even support a videophone link so you can see the person at the other end. In addition to your standard connection to the net, you'll need software that manages the connection. Here are some of the most popular:*

| CuSeeMe | www.cuseeme.com |
| Internet Telephone | www.vocaltec.com |
| Net2Phone | www.net2phone.com |
| Netmeeting | www.microsoft.com |

## Getting the best price

*Use one of these price comparison sites to find an alternative, cheaper supplier for your utilities – switch gas, electricity or water company and save. Specialist sites will compare what's on offer from a range of online shops and point you to the cheapest.*

**Bottom Dollar**                    www.bottomdollar.com
Brilliant US-based site that lets you compare prices on a great range of products (not just the usual books and CDs).

**BuyBuddy**                    www.buybuddy.com
Scour the web for the cheapest place to buy books, computers or home goods.

**buy.co.uk**                    www.buy.co.uk
Find the cheapest source for your utilities – enter your current gas, electricity, water or mobile phone bill to see the local suppliers that could save you money.

**Cheaper Calls UK**                http://cheapercalls.8m.com
Cut the cost of your Orange or One2One mobile phone bills with the help of this provider.

**EvenBetter**                    www.evenbetter.com
Helps find the cheapest book, video or CD on the net market.

**Kura**                    www.kura.co.uk
Save on your gas and electricity by switching supplier.

**MySimon**                    www.mysimon.com
Best of the bunch. Scours a vast range of shops for the cheapest items – with versions for the US and UK.

**Taxi**                              **www.mytaxi.co.uk**
Impressive shopping tool to help find the cheapest book, video or
CD – plus a good directory of shops.

**ShopSmart**                         **www.shopsmart.com**
The bargain finder's guide to the UK – fast, well designed and easy
to use; great for comparing prices of over 90 stores selling books,
videos, games and music.

---

**Cars and vans**

---

**Autobytel.com**                     **www.autobytel.com**
Just about the best place on the net to find a new or used car –
with sections on business tax, leasing, fleet hire and service via an
extensive dealer network.

**AutoExpress**                       **www.autoexpress.co.uk**
Every tiny detail about the latest thing on four wheels. Car-crazy
web addicts can wallow in the vast database of road tests, check
prices, and browse the classifieds (though AutoTrader and
Exchange and Mart are bigger). Use the Links button to get a
directory of the websites for all the major car manufacturers.

**AutoTrader**                        **www.autotrader.co.uk**
Search the thousands of classifieds in an instant – or get an email
when someone advertises your dream car. On a par with archrival
Exchange and Mart.

**British Vehicle and Leasing Association**    **www.bvrla.co.uk**
The trade association that works for the leasing and fleet business
– there's plenty of background information with links to member
sites that can offer you a dozen cars with a click.

**Carsource**                         **www.carsource.co.uk**
Azure blue, tinted glass, alloys and air-con? Use the search system
that matches your requirements with new and used cars available
from main dealers. Once you've found the car, there are links to

insurance companies, lease and finance groups. For used cars, you'll get a better range from AutoTrader and Exchange and Mart.

**Exchange and Mart**  www.exchangeandmart.co.uk
All the classified ads without hunting through the magazine. A simple search function and an email update will ensure you're the first to hear about a new entry. On a par with AutoTrader (www.autotrader.co.uk).

**New Car Net**  www.new-car-net.co.uk
Help choosing your new car. Enter your basic criteria, then compare the models and read in-depth reviews on each. Links to your nearest specialist dealer to complete the deal.

**Vanfinder**  www.vanfinder.co.uk
Want a new 10-tonner or a basic run-around? Not the best example of e-commerce, but it's a start.

**WhatCar?**  www.whatcar.co.uk
A little of everything car-related has been crammed into this informative site. The main features are the road tests but there's also classifieds, used car prices, insurance and finance features.

---

### Commercial property

**The Commercial Network**  www.tcnre.com
Offices and commercial property available around the world – but most of it's in the USA.

**PropShop**  www.dmcsoft.com/propshop/
Efficient, if small, database of commercial properties on offer in Scotland.

**The Property Centre**  www.property-centre.co.uk
Good-looking database of residential and commercial property, with a wide scope across the UK, but very few offices on its books.

**Property Finder**  www.propertyfinder.co.uk
Want a bar, restaurant, hotel or golf club? Together with one of the

biggest residential property databases, there's a mass of niche commercial property available.

**Property Link**  **www.propertylink.co.uk**
Impressive database of offices and commercial property available around the UK.

**Regus**  **www.regus.com**
Rent office space by the day – perfect if you're travelling around the world and need a little peace and quiet with a phone, fax and meeting room.

### Virtual property

*Thanks to the net, you don't need a real office to receive phone calls, faxes, mail or keep in touch with colleagues. Instead, set up a 'virtual office'; companies such as Jfax (www.jfax.com) provide a local telephone number anywhere in the world with an automatic answering service – phone messages and faxes are converted into special files and sent on to you by email.*

## //COMPUTING

It's no surprise that the Internet is packed with resources to help you improve your computer set-up in the office – from choosing a new network to dealing with a troublesome printer. You'll find hundreds of direct suppliers offering low prices, a wide range and all the latest models. If you're not sure what to get, or if it works well, read the ton of product news, reviews and features from online editions of all the computer magazines and compare.

### US suppliers
You'll find the US home to some of the keenest prices and sharpest discounts on new hardware and software. Unfortunately, warranties and guarantees on both rarely extend outside the country. If you're willing to risk this

(you'd normally have to arrange and pay for repairs through a local repair company), you'll probably have to do some sweet-talking to convince them to ship outside the US. Go get 'em.

Once your computer system has been delivered, you'll have to make sure that it's running efficiently. If something goes wrong then, at best, the operator won't be able to work. At worst, they'll lose all their work. To avoid either scenario, look to the websites that help you maintain your software and hardware in tip-top condition. The best place to start is your computer manufacturer's site – to find it, try entering their name or trademark followed by '.com' or '.co.uk'. You'll hit Gateway, Dell, IBM, HP, Elonex, Dan, Time and others in this way. Once you've found your computer's home site, check on updates for essential software drivers that control hard disk, graphics and system board. These are always free to download and could fix some potential bug.

## Starting points

**ZDNet UK**                                          **www.zdnet.co.uk**
Should be any surfer's first stop for computing news, reviews and features from the expert computer magazine publishers. Much of the content is geared towards professional (read business) users, and it's one of the few places where you'll find reviews of accounting software next to website programming tips.

**CNET**                                              **www.cnet.com**
Packed with news, a vast shareware library, advice and step-by-step instructions on everything from building a website to using your software.

## Computer equipment

*Order your custom-built computer from these manufacturers:*

| | |
|---|---|
| **Apple Store** | **www.apple.com** |
| **Dell** | **www.dell.co.uk** |
| **Elonex** | **www.elonex.co.uk** |
| **Evesham Micros** | **www.evesham.com** |
| **Gateway 2000** | **www.gw2k.co.uk** |
| **Viglen** | **www.viglen.co.uk** |

**Action Computer Supplies**      **www.action.com**
Business-oriented hardware, software and accessories supplier. Great service, good prices and a site that's informative and easy to use.

**Download.com**      **www.download.com**
Great library of commercial application software and shareware that you can buy and instantly download to your computer – part of the impressive CNET resource site.

**ECHO Software**      **www.echosoftware.com**
Stretch your buying power and choose second-user software – stacks for sale plus over 100,000 software titles to buy and download directly to your computer.

**Free Site**      **www.thefreesite.com**
Why pay when you can download free software, screensavers and web tools? Also check out **www.filez.com**.

**Inmac**      **www.inmac.co.uk**
Well-stocked warehouse piled high with hardware and software at low prices and with great service.

**Macintouch**      **www.macintouch.com**
Keep your Mac bug-free with the latest software fixes and updates.

**Microwarehouse**      **www.microwarehouse.co.uk**
Provides just about the best range of computer hardware, software

and accessories and all at good prices. Better range than Action, but the search and catalogue is not quite as slick.

**Software Paradise**        **www.softwareparadise.co.uk**
Over 100,000 software titles for sale at discount prices. Covers all platforms from PC to Mac – and from developers around the world. Very easy to use.

**TechWeb**        **www.technweb.com**
Comprehensive database of computer hardware and software that'll help you decide what's best for you.

**Shareware**

*Vast libraries of programs you can download and try out before you pay.*

**CNET**        **www.cnet.com**
Everything you need to know about your PC and the software to make it zing. There's news, lots of reviews, advice on fixing problems and designing websites plus a vast library of shareware.

**Filez**        **www.filez.com**
Claims to have the widest range of shareware files available to download, but CNET wins on general coverage.

**Rocketdownload.com**        **www.rocketdownload.com**
Another good collection of shareware files to download – the big difference here is that the files have all been rated and described (saving you the annoyance of downloading junk).

**TUCOWS network**        **www.tucows.com**
Great collection of all the software you'll ever need – neatly arranged into categories. Rivals CNET in ease of use but without the range of Filez.

**Computer support**

*Once you've installed computers into your office, you'll need to keep them running. If you've over a dozen, someone should take responsibility for maintenance (though they don't have to do it themselves). Almost every computer company offers a wide variety of warranties – for business users, it's worth getting a same-day call-out guarantee, unless you want your office to shut down for a week. And make sure that you've got the latest software updates and bug fixes by using a specialist site or visiting the software publisher's site.*

### Aveo                                                  www.aveo.com
Ditch the IT department. Use this astonishingly clever software that'll warn you if your PC's about to go wrong – and it's free.

### CNET                                                  www.cnet.com
Vast library of technical advice (along with its how-to sections, huge shareware library and industry news).

### DriverZone                                      www.driverzone.com
Drivers are tiny, but vital, bits of software that let your computer control your modem, hard disk, monitor or printer. Check here to make sure you've got the latest version or for advice on problems.

### Help                                            www.free-help.com
Get help fast – ask an expert about your computer problem.

### MacFixIt                                          www.macfixit.com
Help get your Mac working properly (for a change).

### SquareOneTech                               www.squareonetech.com
A useful series of Internet guides that'll tell you almost as much as this book about getting online and using the net – the difference is you first have to work out how to get online to use the guides.

### Updates                                          www.updates.com
Make sure all your applications are up to date – this free utility will scan your hard disk to see what's installed and then it tells you what needs to be updated and how to do it.

What Microsoft didn't include in Windows and how to fix the irritating features they did include.

## //ECONOMICS

The economic climate in your country rates as just about the most important factor in the success of your business. This is especially so if you're planning to export (see page 173), where it's pointless finalising a deal if the interest rates are rocketing sky-high or exchange rates are plummeting.

For British business, the general economic climate tends to be driven by interest rates and the value of sterling – since so much depends upon trade with overseas customers. In the USA, on the other hand, although you probably won't have the time to study economic theories, you should look at summaries of what's happening in government and world news to ensure you have a better understanding of the pressures on your customers and distributors.

To get the best overview of a country's economic outlook, try a specialist website that explains what's happening and why. Government sites are often in the best position to provide an accurate source of information, but they might not want to. Instead, you could try one of the global news sites, such as The Economist (**www.economist.co.uk**), Financial Times (**www.ft.com**) or the OECD (**www.oecd.org**) for an educated (and often opinion-ated) outlook.

But if you've time on your hands and prefer to delve into the theory of economic principles from John Maynard Keynes and other classic economists, visit the resource library at McMaster University in Ontario, Canada (**http://socserv2.socsci.mcmaster.ca/~econ/ugcm**).

**Alan Greenspan**     www.geocities.com/~the-igloo/greenspan/
One enthusiast's very polished website dedicated to just about the most powerful man in world economics – the chairman of the Federal Reserve of the US.

**Australia Department of Treasury**     www.treasury.gov.au
Provides a rundown of the Treasury's activities and the country's economic performance, without the detailed statistics from the US or the wide-ranging consumer reports of the US equivalents.

**The Budget**     www.hm-treasury.gov.uk
What's the British Chancellor got in store for businesses this year? If you want to find anything in the mountain of legislation that makes up the American federal budget, visit **www.access.gpo. gov/omb/**.

**Bureau of Economic Analysis**     www.bea.doc.gov
One of the dullest website designs yet published, but the content (from the US Government's BEA) is gold dust for economists and serious investors.

**CNNfn**     www.cnnfn.com/news/economy/
Concise, accessible summary of world economic news – and the state of the economies themselves – presented with the usual CNN flair.

**Confederation of British Industry**     www.cbi.org.uk
British economic forecasts and the future of local industry.

**The Dismal Scientist**     www.dismalscientist.com
Great range of professional reports on world and market economies, technical analysis and forecasts to help you understand economic trends. Witty graphs and calculators keep it interesting. The site's name derives from the nineteenth-century Scottish historian Thomas Carlyle, who dubbed economics 'the dismal science'.

**Dr Ed Yardeni's Economics Network**     www.yardeni.com
Very clear, thoughtful and highly informed articles on economics

and markets, presented by the chief economist at Deutsche Morgan Grenfell merchant bank.

### DTI (The Department of Trade and Industry)    www.dti.gov.uk
Official news and regulations with their economic implications clearly written for consumers, investors and business people.

### The Economist                          www.economist.co.uk
Vastly influential weekly comment and analysis of world economic events. Keep up to date with free online access to the latest issues.

### The Economist Intelligence Unit              www.eiu.com
Current reports on world economic trends available to browse, but the real gold mine – the database of past reports – is a chargeable extra. Try the Statistical data locators site as a free alternative.

### Euromoney                              www.euromoney.com
Worthy if soporific articles on the economies and market conditions of European countries, with plenty of links to websites covering specific topics.

### Federal Reserve Bank                      www.stls.frb.org
By the banks of the Mississippi in St Louis stands the nation's bank – often seen as the target for daring movie exploits. Its website provides plenty of educational and informational material about the US and the bank's role, together with economic reports and analysis.

### Financial Times                            www.ft.com
Vast (free) archive of world news and features and their impact on markets and economies.

### FinWeb                                www.finweb.com
Despite the name, nothing to do with fish – but plenty of links and features from academic journals and papers. A fascinating, if cerebral, view of current economic and market analysis.

### HM Treasury                        www.hm-treasury.gov.uk
The official line on the UK budget, economy, trends, savings and lots of numbers.

**International Monetary Fund**   www.imf.org
An often bleak view of the state of various countries, world economics, poverty, debt relief and how the IMF (and its member states) can help.

**Morgan Stanley**   www.ms.com
Global reports from each office of the vast broker provide a sharp, accurate summary of the economic trends and forecasts for that country.

**The National Institute of Economic**   www.
**and Social Research**   niesr.ac.uk
Reports, forecasts and analysis of our social and economic future – but you'll have to pay to view.

**Organisation for Economic**   www.
**Co-operation and Development**   oecd.org
Tucked away in here are statistics on just about everything from agriculture to education – spanning almost every country.

**Resources for Economists**   http://rfe.wustl.edu/
**on the Web**   EconFAQ.html
Comprehensive directory of sites listing everything an economist could want – from complex software applications to forecasts and research papers. Great for brave investors.

**Scottish Executive Reports**   www.scotland.gov.uk
The relatively new Scottish Executive provides the latest news and figures on the local economic and political landscape.

**Statistical data locators**   www.ntu.edu.sg/library/statdata.htm
No design, simple presentation but a vast resource that lists economic information about almost every world economy including the latest budgets, statistical data and economic forecasts.

**Stat-USA**   www.stat-usa.gov
Provided by the US Department of Commerce, this is the best place to find economic, business and trade figures, forecasts and analysis.

**Treasury Worldwide**         **www.treasuryworldwide.com**
The first page, with its table of effective bank base rates for the major countries of the world, makes terrifying or comforting reading, depending on where you live.

**USA Today Quarterly**         **www.usatoday.com/money/**
**Economic Survey**         **economy/econ0001.htm**
The national newspaper's regular summary of the state of the US economy.

**US Census Bureau   www.census.gov/cgi-bin/briefroom/BriefRm**
Clear, clean page of graphs that tell you exactly what's happened in the US economy – from home sales to retail trade.

**The Virtual Economy**         **http://ve.ifs.org.uk**
Impressive set of sophisticated tools to help you model your own economy – based on the same calculations and figures used by Britain's Chancellor of the Exchequer to work out his own real-life budgets.

**World Bank**         **www.worldbank.org**
All about this vast organisation and its aims, plus analysis of economies and research. Find out how it helps to fund the world's poorest countries – and perhaps save them from disaster.

## //FINANCIAL MANAGEMENT

Access your account details over the Internet, transfer money, pay bills, even sort out insurance and pensions. Just about every bank now provides Internet access to their current accounts – and with its low overheads and automated structure, most banks would love it if everyone switched overnight.

In the US, almost every bank provides full-service Internet access. In the UK, some of the bigger banks, notably Barclays, describe a future in which almost all their account holders will switch to Internet access within the next few years. Consumers have an even more complex choice with the arrival of virtual banks, such as Smile (www.smile.co.uk) and First-e (www.first-e.com), which operate only via the Internet – though neither Smile nor First-e will yet accept business customers.

If you plan to open a new account, you'll still need to visit your local branch to explain your business plan (see page 126 for details on creating a killer plan) and haggle over an overdraft limit. Once terms have been agreed, you'll have to sign paperwork but then, with the exception of the yearly visit from the business manager, you can carry out almost every transaction over the net. But do read the section on security and firewalls (page 13) or you might provide full access to your bank account to all your staff.

---

## Starting points

**AAAdir Directory**                     **www.aaadir.com**
Who would have thought there were so many? From Andorra to Yugoslavia, a directory of thousands of banks and their websites listed by country.

**Bank Rate Monitor**                    **www.bankrate.com**
Compiles the latest rates for accounts, loans and credit cards – so that you can find the best deal in the US.

**Mark Bernkopf's**               **www.adams.patriot.net/**
**Central Banking Resource**            **~bernkopf/**
Good directory of international banks, financial institutions, mints – even national banknote printers.

**PayMyBills**                          **www.paymybills.com**
Type in details of your company's phone and utility bills and, if you're in the US, this service will make sure that they're paid on time.

---

## Business banking

**Adelaide Bank**                  **www.adelaidebank.com.au**
Full Internet access to your account in Australia.

**Allied Irish Bank**                                   **www.aib.ie**

Full Internet banking facilities with a clear, friendly interface that makes it very easy to use. So easy, in fact, that it's won awards.

**Bank of America**                          **www.bankofamerica.com**

In common with those of many US banks, customers can choose to get efficient, full-service banking from the Internet, via AOL, by direct-dial connection, by phone or – for the truly radical – by visiting a local branch.

**Bank of England**                          **www.bankofengland.co.uk**

What's going on inside Britain's central bank.

**Bank of Melbourne**                       **www.bankmelb.com.au**

Makes it very straightforward for any customer to get full access to their account via the net.

**The Bank of New York**                      **www.bankofny.com**

East-coast North Americans bank here. Preferably with a bagel with lox next to their keyboards.

**Bank of Scotland**             **www.bankofscotland.co.uk/business**

One of the oldest British banks and one of the first to provide online access from this friendly site.

**Barclays Business Banking**          **www.business.barclays.co.uk**

Convinced that almost all its customers will be on the net within a year, Barclays has invested heavily in its full-service banking.

**Chase Manhattan Bank**                       **www.chase.com**

Online banking aimed at New York's rich – though any super-rich customers are welcome. You can download your data and manage your online account using Microsoft Money or Intuit Quicken.

**Citibank**                                   **www.citibank.com**

Perfect for jetsetters – online access to a choice of sterling, Euro or dollar accounts.

**Co-operative Bank**            www.co-operativebank.co.uk
Good for small businesses and cash accounting – with full Internet access to your account.

**Federal Reserve**            www.federalreserve.gov
News, economic forecasts and comment from the US central bank. Rather dry, but you'd hardly expect jokes from this lot.

**Girobank**            www.girobank.co.uk
With a branch in every Post Office, it's local and good with cash-based accounts.

**HSBC Group**            www.hsbcgroup.com
Great believers in the web and interactive-TV banking experience; either way, you can check your account online.

**Lloyds TSB**            www.lloydstsb.co.uk
Smart, efficient site provides full Internet access to your business account.

**NatWest**            www.natwest.co.uk
Full Internet access to your current account and credit card details.

**Reserve Bank of Australia**            www.rba.gov.au
Gives away just the bare essentials about the official economic outlook for Australia.

**Royal Bank of Scotland**            www.rbos.co.uk
Full-function Internet banking that's easy to use. In case you get bored staring at your balance, there are masses of briefings on economic indicators, forecasts and nifty financial calculators.

**South African Reserve Bank**            www.resbank.co.za
Hardly dynamic, but it does include all the national economic news.

**Standard Chartered Bank**            www.stanchart.com
Worldwide bank provides business accounts, but only via its few high-street branches.

**Ulster Bank Group**  www.ulsterbank.com
Online banking for Irish or British businesses.

**Wells Fargo**  www.wellsfargo.com
The name may be redolent of the old Wild West, but the site is
bang up to date with full Internet access to accounts.

---

### Factoring

*One way to get paid on time is to keep a pack of wild dogs ready
to hound late payers. A more practical approach is to use a
factoring or invoice discounting company. You hand over the
invoicing and collection part of your business, they generate the
invoices, pay you a large chunk of the money on invoicing, then
the rest once they have collected the money from the customer.
You lose control of your invoices, but your cashflow improves
dramatically.*

**Alex Lawrie**  www.alexlawrie.com
The biggest name on other people's invoices in the UK. They take
over your invoicing and credit control department to make sure
that you get the invoice value on time.

**Associated Risk Consultants**  www.riskconsult.co.uk
Worried about bad debts and selling goods on invoice to unknown
or potentially risky companies? Instead of factoring your entire
invoice system, use a specialist to provide help organising credit
insurance, factoring, bonds or, if it goes wrong, debt recovery.

**Bank of New York Co**  www.bankofny.com
One of the biggest collection and factoring banks that, like all
good US banks, provides help collecting money owed, financing
invoices (factoring) or working out a system to improve cashflow
and reduce risk.

**Credit and Debt Collection**  www.insolvency.co.uk/credit
The site's mainly concerned with companies on the verge of
bankruptcy, but tucked away here there's a good list of links to

debt collection agencies, insurance companies and factoring services for companies that would rather not go bust.

**Credit Lyonnais Commercial Finance Ltd**   **www.clcf.co.uk**
The vast French bank provides a range of financing products for UK companies to help improve their cashflow using its factoring solution, or taking out one of their short-term business loans.

**Gaelic Invoice Factors Ltd.**   **www.gaelic-factors.co.uk**
Improve cashflow by transferring your invoicing and collection to this specialist factoring company that will ensure you get paid on time.

**Griffin Services**   **www.griffincs.co.uk**
Like all high-street banks, HSBC has a specialist business group that offers invoice discounting, factoring and credit management for its business customers.

---

### Bankruptcy

---

*The Internet reaches everywhere – even to the bankruptcy courts. If your business is suffering a worrying cashflow crisis, and you don't want to face your partners or bank manager, you can get advice from the websites below and, with luck, you will be able to avoid the unpleasantness of an insolvency hearing. If, however, it's all got way out of hand and the only solution is to go bust, you can use your computer (don't forget it's another company asset that'll be sold off, along with this book) to help you understand what happens next.*

**About.com**   **http://credit.about.com/finance/credit/mbody.htm**
Borrowing getting out of hand? Good advice on credit management.

**Bankruptcy FAQ**   **www.agin.com/bkfaq/**
Answers to your questions about bankruptcy and debt – covers assets, attorneys and dealing with creditors.

**Bankruptcy Terms**	www.abiworld.org/media/terms.html
It's hard enough dealing with bankruptcy without having to struggle with the jargon. Use this useful glossary from the American Bankruptcy Institute.

**Credit.com**	www.credit.com
Plenty of practical resources for anyone with debt problems.

**InterNet Bankruptcy Library**	www.bankrupt.com
A clear, sensible directory of companies that can help you wind-up and manage a bankruptcy.

---

**Loans and finance**

---

*If you want to borrow money for growth or capital purchase, there's a whole range of places that could provide finance. Your bank is probably the most likely to say yes, simply because you already have a track record and relationship. However, they might not provide the best terms for the loan, so you could try out your business plan on a range of other lenders first – then turn to your bank. You should also try local advice centres that'll have alternative contacts for finance, such as the Business Link centres (www.businesslink.co.uk). And if you're planning to raise millions, fund a takeover or stock flotation, talk to one of the venture capital companies.*

**EquipmentLeasing.com**	www.equipmentleasing.com
Not hard to figure out this site – you find the equipment, they arrange the lease.

**Find.co.uk**	www.find.co.uk
Good directory of lenders offering business (and personal) loans.

**iii**	www.iii.co.uk
Data-driven financial megasite that lets you check the current interest rate movements – and how they impact on loans.

**GE Capital**　　　　www.ge.com/capital/smallbiz/financial.htm
Financing deals for small businesses, from the deep investment pockets of General Electric.

**IBM Financing**　　　　　　　　**www.ibm.com/financing/**
The big blue provides finance deals for companies to help expand – or buy new computers.

**LeaseAdvisor**　　　　　　　　**www.leaseadvisor.com**
Helps you plan the best way to get equipment and grow your business through leasing. Online tools let you check the costs as you surf.

**LiveCapital**　　　　　　　　**www.livecapital.com**
Want a business loan? Apply and get a decision in five minutes.

**vCapital**　　　　　　　　**www.vcapital.com**
Lots of advice to help perfect your business plan, then a panel of 150 VC lenders who'll assess if they want to advance a loan.

**Venture Capital Resources**　　　　**www.vfinance.com**
A great place to start if you're considering VC. Good guides to what's involved, how to pitch and a directory of links to companies that have deep pockets.

**Venture-Capitalist.com**　　　　**www.venture-capitalist.com**
No fuss, no frills, just lots of guides and advice to help get a chunk of venture capital money to fund your company – with an invaluable online database of likely targets.

**Merrill Lynch**　　　　　　**http://businesscenter.ml.com**
Business loans and financing for American companies that plan to expand.

**Autobytel**　　　　　　　　**www.autobytel.co.uk**
Check for the best loan deals direct from car manufacturers.

**Salomon Smith Barney**     www.salomonsmithbarney.com/ prod_svc/business/

Want to fund a takeover or borrow a lot? This merchant bank can help with most high-finance deals.

**3i Corporate Finance**     www.3i.com

Just about the best-known investment firm in the UK will consider advancing money against a share of the company – if the terms and forecasts are favourable.

**NatWest Acquisition Finance**     www.nwacqfin.com

Want to buy your rival? NatWest might provide the funds.

---

### Grants

---

*If you want to buy new equipment, move premises or invest in staff training? If you do, there might well be a grant available to help you out. There are several sources: trading bodies (such as the EU), national governments, local and regional councils and (rich) philanthropic individuals and their foundations. In the US, most of the grants and financial aid is geared towards students and education (although there are exceptions); in the UK there are grants to help relocate your business to a deprived area or to make capital purchases. And of course there's the renowned cash-cow, the EU. It has plenty of grants on offer, but finding out about them and managing the application process can be a slow and bothersome business – luckily there are specialist companies on offer who can tell you if there's something out there to help you.*

**1066 Enterprise**     www.1066.sussexenterprise.co.uk/grants.htm

Hard up in Hastings? Ignore the awful name, this local business site, provided by the regional borough council, lists grants for training, relocation and development available for local businesses. It's a good example of what's on offer for local companies – use the search for your local council with Local Government (**www.local. doe.gov.uk**).

**Alfred P. Sloan Foundation**  www.sloan.org

The late boss of General Motors set up this fund to help improve social issues, technology and education – it's got over $1bn in reserves and a wide range of programmes on offer.

**Combined Heat and Power Association**  www.chpa.co.uk

Turn down the thermostat and switch off the lights. But if you'd rather not wear thermals in the office or work in the dark, you can use the advice and information from this organisation to locate grants to help insulate office walls and ensure your building's energy efficient.

**Eurofi**  www.eurofi.co.uk

Get a slice of EU dosh – with the help of this advisory consultant; and if there's no grant currently available, sign up for their email service to be the first to hear if Brussels has opened its purse.

**GrantsNet**  www.grantsnet.org

Interested in advancing your medical or biological expertise? There's plenty of funding available on this database of specialist grants.

**The Harrison Partnership**  www.thp.uk.com

If there's a UK government grant available to help you with training, relocation or development, these folk will know about it – and can help you get it.

**IREX**  www.irex.org

Thinking of improving your knowledge of business Mongolian or travel to Ulaanbataar? This organisation might be able to help with research and funding – yes, it's specialist, but you'll have a unique skill.

---

**Pensions**

---

*In many countries, including Britain, current legislation forces all companies to provide some form of pension for employees.*

*This can be as simple as a basic framework to allow people to choose their own pension plans, but it does still have to be in place. All of the major pension providers will provide pension products that comply with current regulations, or use these sites for advice, help and ways to find the best-performing pension on offer.*

**The 401(k)**                                    **www.the401k.com**
News and plenty of opinions for and against (though generally for) the 401(k) pension schemes in the US.

**The 401(k)**                            **http://401kcenter.com/**
**15-second summary**                              **summary.htm**
Concise guides to retirement planning using the common, if often criticised, 401(k) vehicle.

**Blay's Guides**                              **www.blays.co.uk**
Excellent set of guides to help plan your pension – and the rest of your finances.

**DSS (Department of Social Security)**        **www.dss.gov.uk**
Get the latest official news on how you, as a business, should provide a pension framework and, for employees, chilling news on the very meagre state pension you can expect when you retire.

**FIND**                                      **www.find.co.uk**
Thinking of offering a company pension to the team? Here's a directory of online pension advisers, suppliers and brokers who can help you out.

**Micropal**                              **www.micropal.com**
Check what the leading worldwide pension-rating company thinks of your fund.

**MoneyeXtra**                          **www.moneyextra.com**
News and tools to help compare and choose the best pension on offer.

## Pension companies

*Keep up to date with the latest news (and value) of your pension scheme – visit the administrating company's website.*

| | |
|---|---|
| **Clerical Medical** | **www.clericalmedical.co.uk** |
| **The Equitable Life** | **www.equitable.co.uk** |
| **Friends Provident** | **www.friendsprovident.co.uk** |
| **Legal and General** | **www.landg.com** |
| **National and Mutual** | **www.nationalmutual.co.uk** |
| **Norwich Union** | **www.norwich-union.co.uk** |
| **Prudential** | **www.prudential.co.uk** |
| **Royal Liver Insurance** | **www.royal-liver.com** |
| **Scottish Widows** | **www.scottishwidows.co.uk** |
| **Standard Life** | **www.standardlife.co.uk** |
| **Virgin Direct** | **www.virgin-direct.co.uk** |

## Credit cards

*Credit cards are the perfect way to manage business expenses, delay the cost of a purchase or pay for goods on the Internet. Instead of issuing dozens of cheques each month, the accounts department can manage a single bill for the card, and get an itemised statement in return.*

*Most businesses will probably pay off the card each month, simply using it to extend credit for this month. In this case, the interest rate is of no particular concern. Instead, you can look at some of the other impressive deals on offer – such as cashback or frequent flyer points. Use a comparison tool such as MoneyeXtra (**www.moneyextra.co.uk/products/credit_cards.asp**) to compare the latest charges and rates. If an Internet card looks better than your old plastic (and it probably will), apply online for an instant decision. Unfortunately, many of the best deals are for consumers only, so you might have to hunt awhile before finding a business-friendly card.*

**Aria** www.aria.com

It's finally here – an Internet-based credit card with a zero rate of interest. But you've got to be a US resident.

**BankOne** www.bankone-uk.com

One of the biggest card-issuing banks with an Internet credit card offering very low interest rates.

**CapitalOne** www.capitalone.co.uk

Gold? Pah! Here's an online platinum card with money-off deals.

**Charity Credit Card** www.charitycard.co.uk

Save as you spend – apply online for a card that gives money to charities (such as Battersea Dogs' Home) as you use your credit card.

**Egg** www.egg.com

Internet-only card offers low interest rates, a guarantee for stuff bought online and cashback incentives. It's a popular site, so loading can be painfully slow.

**Goldfish** www.goldfish.com

Save money from your utility bills whenever you use the card. From the people behind Marbles.

**i-Circle** www.icircle.co.uk

Helps find the best credit-card deals around at the moment – together with tables of the top investment, tax and financial products.

**Marbles** www.getmarbles.co.uk

Internet credit card with low interest rates and a guarantee when you're shopping online.

**Moneynet** www.moneynet.co.uk

Choose the perfect credit card. Fill in a form and you'll be sent details of dozens of deals.

**Novus**  www.novusnet.com

Huge in the US with its Discover card, but has yet to catch on in the UK.

## Card companies

| | |
|---|---|
| **AmericanExpress** | www.americanexpress.com |
| **DinersClub** | www.dinersclub.com |
| **MasterCard** | www.mastercard.com |
| **Visa** | www.visa.com |

## Insurance Brokers

*Run a business? You need insurance – for your buildings, stock, employee liability, health, bad debt, travel and fleet of company limousines. Use the net to help you find a business-friendly broker (most of the online brokers are oriented towards personal insurance clients) or do the work yourself with an automated comparison tool that'll help you choose the cheapest insurance policy around.*

**Ault Insurance Brokers**  www.jsault.demon.co.uk

Find the best deal for your business, property or risk-based insurance from this specialist broker.

**Ben McArdle**  www.benmcardle.ie/

Worried about debt risk or want corporate or personnel insurance? This Dublin-based broker will try to get the best deal.

**Business Insurance Online**  www.businessinsurance.com

Responsible for insurance and risk in your company? If so, the high-level news and features will keep you up to date.

**British Insurance &**  www.biiba.
**Investment Broker's Association**  org.uk

Find a local broker that specialises in your corporate risk requirements.

**Chatburns**                                   www.chatburns.co.uk
Specialist broker that aims to get you a good deal on your public liability, professional or corporate insurance – or your fleet of cars.

**CIC Insurance**                               www.cicinsurance.co.uk
Brokers who can help find the best policy to protect your office, employees, risk or equipment.

**FIND**                                        www.find.co.uk
Clear financial directory with dozens of insurance sites covering home, pet, car and travel insurance brokers and companies that are online.

**Moody's Investors Service**        www.moodys.com/insurance
Highly respected rating company gives you the low-down on the top insurance providers and policies.

### General insurance

**Axa Direct**                                  www.axa.co.uk
Basic background information on the policies on offer.

**Churchill Insurance**                         www.churchill.co.uk
Get a competitive quote online from this leading direct seller.

**Cornhill Direct**                             www.cornhilldirect.co.uk
Wide range of products – including business and employee insurance.

**Eagle Star Insurance**                        www.eaglestardirect.co.uk
Get a quote and buy your policy online.

**Hill House Hammond**                          www.hhh.co.uk
Insure just about anything through these brokers.

**iii (Interactive Investor International)**       www.iii.co.uk
Clear design leads you straight to the best guides and quotes for car and travel insurance.

**The Insurance News Network**     www.insure.com
Nice web address, great site – provides a comprehensive guide to
all types of insurance, with stacks on insurance policies, ratings and
quotes.

**Insurance Online**     www.insure.net
Find your nearest broker in the US.

**MoneyeXtra**     www.moneyextra.co.uk
Compare car or travel insurance policies to find the best deal for
your requirements.

**National Association of Insurance Commissioners** www.naic.org
The organisation charged with keeping law and order in the US
insurance industry – a good place to find help getting a decent
adviser, or complaining about a bad one.

**Royal & Sun Alliance**     www.royal-and-sunalliance.com
One of the biggest global investment companies provides a wide
range of insurance products, from healthcare to home contents
and pets – get instant quotes online.

**Screen Trade**     www.screentrade.co.uk
Reduce your insurance bill by comparing umpteen different
suppliers – for car and travel.

**Yahoo! Insurance**     http://insurance.yahoo.com
Fill in your details to get an instant comparison of quotes from the
leading insurers.

---

**Motor insurance**

---

*Use a specialist insurance supplier, or visit a car website to check
for details on special deals and offers from manufacturers.*

**The AA**     www.theaa.com
Yes, the yellow vans help when you've broken down – but they'll
also provide standard car insurance.

**Admiral**  www.admiral.uk.com
Cheap car insurance on offer.

**Autobytel.co.uk**  www.autobytel.co.uk
Car supersite provides plenty of information on insurance policies.

**Belair Direct**  www.belairdirect.com
Canadian drivers can buy instant cover online from this insurance company.

**Carsource**  www.carsource.co.uk
Lets you choose your new car and an insurance policy to match.

**CGU Direct**  www.cgu-direct.co.uk
Get a quote online, but you'll need to phone up before you're covered.

**Cornhill Direct**  www.cornhilldirect.co.uk/van
Got a van? Insure it here.

**GEICO**  www.geico.com
Get an instant quote and then buy your policy online from GEICO, one of the biggest direct providers.

**Insure.com**  www.insure.com/auto
Clear guides to the basics about auto insurance – together with chat forums to dish the dirt on less scrupulous providers, and tables of crash-test results that explain why your premiums are so high.

**Ironsure**  www.ironsure.com
Scan a range of suppliers for the cheapest online quotes to insure your motor.

**Norwich Union Direct**  www.norwichunion.co.uk
The vast insurance and investment group provides basic information on most of its products, but for car insurance you can get quotes and buy cover online.

**Privilege Insurance**                    www.privilege.co.uk
Likes to insure big or fast cars – but you'll have to resort to the phone to get cover.

**Pru Auto Discounts**        www.prudential.com/insurance/auto
Step through the online questionnaire and the Pru will provide advice and simple quotes for your next auto insurance policy.

**WhatCar?**                          www.whatcar.co.uk
Car-magazine supersite that provides features and links to car insurance sites.

---

**Medical insurance**

---

**About.com – Health Care Industry**   http://healthcare.about.com
Impressive guide to the entire healthcare insurance subject – with features and commentary on the industry and links to sites and brokers.

**Aetna US Healthcare**                   www.aetnaushc.com
Just about the biggest healthcare provider in the US offers up a useful site where you can buy your next policy online.

**Blue Cross**                         www.bluecross.com
The most recognised name in US healthcare insurance.

**BUPA**                              www.bupa.co.uk
One of the nicest sites in the sector, with masses of information, news and, naturally, plugs for their private health insurance. Click a button and they'll phone you to discuss the options.

**Health Plan Directory**           www.healthplandirectory.com
The title leaves little to the imagination, and it's no surprise to find it houses a directory of healthcare providers in the US.

**Legal and General**                 www.landg.com/health/
**Healthcare**                          health1.html
Bright, friendly website answers all your questions. If you answer a few of theirs you'll get a tailored information pack through the post.

**Medibroker**                     **www.medibroker.co.uk**
Independent broker specialising in health insurance. Picks out the best and cheapest match from a wide range of insurers and provides quotes by return of email.

**Norwich Union**                     **www.norwich-union.co.uk**
Clear, simple design tells you what's available and then directs you to a freephone number.

**PPP**                     **www.ppphealthcare.co.uk**
A smart, purposeful site from one of Britain's major medical insurers, with news for existing members, descriptions of the plans to enthuse non-members and health information for anyone who's unwell.

**XShealth**                     **www.xshealth.co.uk**
Futuristic design from one of the few UK Internet-based medical insurers (actually part of the well-established WPA group). You can get a quote or buy insurance online – or get advice from the online doctor.

## //GLOBAL BUSINESS AND EXPORTS

So the Internet provides a global market ripe for the export of your goods and services. Now what? In this section, we cover the sites that help you research a country, find and forge relationships with new partners, then check local business etiquette to ensure you export your products and services successfully.

To help you assess a new country, look to reports produced by the British Council, or your own government trade department. These might also offer lists of potential contacts, official requests for tender and even, as with the British Council, a daily email service to keep you in touch with niche trade sectors. The one country that has little information to help potential importers is the USA. Since the majority of the Internet world centres on the USA, it assumes that the majority of business people online must also be American – hence they're looking for export markets outside the States.

If you think that you can sell your products overseas but are not sure how to do it, there's plenty of advice on the business megasites as well as in the discussion forums of business magazines (see page 102). To speak to a real person, rather than shout across the net, talk to your local Business Link centre.

Before you arrive in the country with a suitcase full of samples, take the time to look at the local products, customs and market conditions. There's no point selling luxury goods to a country barely able to repay its national debt. However, they might have a World Bank grant to improve education – good for anyone trying to sell educational material. Similarly, if you export to a local distributor, they'll probably mark up your prices and sales could suffer. Get educated to the local market and search out products similar to your own to check local pricing, then set prices and discounts with your distributor for a better chance at competing with local producers.

If you want to make a good impression, make sure that your website and sales material is available in the local language – don't just stick to English. To help you translate emails, letters and texts, try Babelfish (http://babelfish.altavista.com) and you'll get a free translation that's accurate enough to at least understand the gist of the message.

## Starting points

**Big Emerging Markets Information Resource Page**　　　　www.ita.doc. gov/bems

Want to trade with Brazil or South Korea? Both are covered in this excellent, if starkly designed, resource from the US Department of Commerce. You'll find background briefings on the dozen-odd countries listed, notes on protocol and hints to help you conquer.

**British Council**　　　　www.britcoun.org

Packed with country-specific reports, contacts and export

opportunities, this should be your first stop. Most countries have a local British Council office that can also help with specific questions – such as 'Do you know a local lawyer?' Some industries also get a daily email service that provides notes on tender requests, trade shows and local news.

### British Trade International          www.brittrade.com
A friendly, well-designed and useful place to start looking for ideas, leads and information about export markets. Funded by the British government.

### Central Europe Online          www.centraleurope.com
Efficient portal that gathers together news, financial headlines, company reports, and background detail on the main countries in Central Europe.

### Company Annual Reports On-Line (CAROL)     www.carol.co.uk
Worried about a new customer? Check the annual report of companies in the UK, Asia and Europe to make sure they're not in the red. Originally aimed at investors, there are no credit ratings, but it's free and a useful first step.

### Corporate Location          www.corporatelocation.com
Impressive mass of information about 200 countries – and for less adventurous American companies, it also covers the 50 US states. Based on the text from the eponymous magazine, you can search articles, comment, economy briefings and view maps.

### The Economist Intelligence Unit          www.eiu.com
Current reports on world economic trends available to browse, but the real gold mine – the database of past reports – is a chargeable extra. Try the Statistical data locators site (see below) as a free alternative.

### Emerging Markets Companion          www.emgmkts.com
Just about every scrap of news, market report, index and analysis is packed into this great site – and it's free.

**EMU Net**                                    www.euro-emu.co.uk
Still wondering how the Euro will change your business life? Here's
one of the most complete accounts of what's happening, why and
what it all means. For a more business-centric view, try the
*Financial Times* archive of articles (www.ft.com/emu).

**Hieros Gamos/Lex Mundi**                          www.hg.org/
**Business Guides**                                  guides.html
What do you get if you put 150 law firms together on the web? An
astonishingly useful range of concise, pertinent guides to countries
and states, together with a directory of links to other business and
legal guides online. And, best of all, it's free.

**HUGIN**                                      www.huginonline.com
Keep up to date with your competitors all over Euroland – this news
service reports on companies and their activities across Europe.

**International Monetary Fund (IMF)**              www.imf.org
Dry but fascinating documents covering the economic problems
and principles of just about every world country.

**The Internationalist**                  www.internationalist.com
Get help with your international endeavours – advice on business
and business travel around the world.

**Statistical data locators**    www.ntu.edu.sg/library/statdata.htm
Jones, I want a full report on the viability of opening an office
in Venezuela. Here's a great site for anyone researching a new
territory; it has economic information about every world economy.

**Worldly Investor**                      www.worldlyinvestor.com
Aimed at investors, it's packed with information about stocks and
shares, but the background details are great: country-by-country
reports on local conditions, economies and indicators give you a
broad overview of the state of the nation – before you start a major
export drive.

## Fonts

If you can't print the Euro symbol, it probably means that your computer pre-dates its conception. If you've got Windows 95 or earlier, you'll need a special font or patch – available free from Microsoft (**www.microsoft.com/europe/euro/**). If you're trying to view pages with script and characters from a different non-roman language, you'll need a new font – it will download automatically.

## Africa

**Africa Online**                                    **www.africaonline.co.ke**
Deals and high finance from Ghana, Kenya, Tanzania and the rest of Africa. A heady mix of local daily and business news makes this the best way to keep up with this vast continent.

**Coconet:**                                         **http://africa-**
**Ivory Coast**               **info.ihost.com/pages/2ci/ann0800.htm**
Need to contact a bank or find a potential partner in the Ivory Coast? Just about the only site, and a very basic one at that, offering a list of contact details for the country, organised by industry.

**Guyana News and Information**          **www.guyana.org**
Encouragement, support and advice for any business interested in investing in Guyana or working with a local company.

**i Pages**                                          **www.ipages.co.za**
Directory of South African businesses on the web.

**KenyaWeb**                                         **www.kenyaweb.com**
Stacks of information about the Kenyan economy, government and business climate wrapped around a central directory of local business contacts.

## Asia

### Asia Business Connection (ABC)     www.asiabiz.com
A great place to start finding out about Asia and the entire Pacific-rim region with stacks of advice, guides and a directory of importers and exporters, business services and hotels and travel.

### Asia Inc.     www.asia-inc.com
Bills itself as the portal to business in Asia – it's still under development but will provide a range of articles and features from the print magazine of the same name together with business and economic news.

### Asia-Pacific Economic Cooperation (APEC)   www.apecsec.org.sg
The Asia-Pacific countries together form one of the fastest growing economies of the world – and this organisation was set up to promote trade between and with them. You'll find dry, but useful, briefings and features on the economic and business climates in each country, together with directories of links to country-specific resources. A good if slightly dull place to start.

### Bank of Japan     www.boj.or.jp/en
Serious business visitors and economists only need visit this stark presentation of facts and figures from the National Bank – great fun if you want to know the day's official uncollaterised call rate average – whatever that might be.

### BPS Statistics Indonesia     www.bps.go.id
Clean presentation of the basic facts behind the economic and business functions of Indonesia. Good as for an overview, but you'll need to contact the department directly if you want specific export information.

### China External Trade     www.tptaiwan.
### Development Council     org.tw
Impressive mass of news, features and financial information, clearly presented within this portal to Taiwan business. Includes plenty of

worthy economic data plus guides for visiting business people – on how to tip and local business practice.

**China Infobank Limited**  www.chinainfobank.com
Financial, political and business news from China (and Hong Kong and Taiwan) as it happens – if you want to read all of the main home page, you'll need to download the special font plug-in for your browser, otherwise click on 'Realtime China' and move straight to the news feed.

**China Web**  www.comnex.com
Mishmash of business, weather, economic and share information backed up with a directory of local business contacts. Most interesting are its profiles of the power players in the government and industry.

**China Window**  http://china-window.com
One of the smartest sites around presents information on exports, local business, news on tourism and culture together with guides on doing business with a Chinese company.

**ChinaPages**  www.chinapages.com
Surrounding its main directory of local companies, organised by sector, there's business and niche industry news and a discussion forum where you can ask for or offer products and services.

**ECCP Online**  www.eccp.com
Want to do business with the Philippines? This organisation was set up to help European and Philippine companies get together. There's information about trade shows, local business opportunities and help with import and export.

**Far Eastern Economic Review (FEER)**  www.feer.com
Great features and news from the journalists hard at work covering business within the Far East. You'll find articles on current investment trends, market conditions and business news from the many countries in the area.

**Federation of Indian Export Organisations (FIEO)  www.fieo.com**
Direct access to over 100,000 exporting companies scattered across
India – plus vital information on the strict tax and import/export
laws.

**Federation of Pakistan Chambers                              www.fpcci.**
**of Commerce and Industry                                          com**
One of the few sites covering Pakistan provides a well-presented
business resource for travellers (hotels, airlines, business agencies)
and basic advice if you're interested in finding and working with a
local partner company.

**Hong Kong                                www.info.gov.hk/mardep/**
**Shipping Directory                              sdfiles/shipdir.htm**
If you want to move goods to and from Hong Kong, you'll need to
use a shipper – and this site's got the lot, from shipyards to freight
forwarders, maritime insurance to specialist banks.

**Hong Kong Statistics          www.info.gov.hk/censtatd/**
Dull but useful numbers that together make up the Hong Kong
economy and population. Ideal fodder if you're planning a
presentation or wondering if there are enough people on the
island to afford your goods.

**Hong Kong Trade Development Council      www.tdctrade.com**
The best place to find out just about anything business-related
from Hong Kong. The site's packed with data on niche business
news and trade shows, together with sections for trading partners
– or sign up for free email delivery of breaking business news.

**India                                    www.indiaintl.com**
Nice, simple name hides a comprehensive, informative site that
covers all aspects of doing business in India.

**India Invest                              www.india-invest.com**
Want to pump money into India? Here's the latest news and
opportunities on offer.

### IndiaMART
www.indiamart.com

How to start up import or export with an Indian partner – and travel guides to make sure you're comfortable when you visit.

### Indian Economy and Business Links
www.ib-net.com/links/economy.htm

Where to find a bank or business in India; hardly exciting stuff, but essential when doing business.

### Japan External Trade Organisation (JETRO), London
www.jetro.co.uk

Promotes and supports trade with Japan through three dozen local offices; there's information on how to trade and how JETRO can help your business.

### Japan Financials
http://japanfinancials.com

Mad on numbers? Here's a database with thousands of spreadsheets and financial reports from all the major Japanese businesses, government departments and law firms filed since 1983. Love it or hate it, it's impressive. For more general statistics on Japan, its population and culture, use the equally number-crazed Japan Information Network (www.jinjapan.org/stat/).

### Nikkei Net Interactive
www.nni.nikkei.co.jp

Japan's foremost English-language business newspaper is the source for this excellent site, which provides local market news, features, stock prices, analysis, trends and company profiles. Subscription-based, but well worth it.

---

### Australasia

---

### ANZlink Limited
www.nzlink.com

Set up down-under with help from this support site linking business people in Australia, New Zealand and the UK; and if you're stuck for an idea, there's advice and a database of business opportunities on offer.

**Australian Business Limited**                    **www.abol.net**
Business news and features, aimed at businesses in Australia, but useful for anyone interested in keeping up with the latest from Oz. Includes news on new contracts and awards, guides to management techniques and general business advice.

**Australian Chamber of**                          **www.acci.**
**Commerce and Industry**                          **asn.au**
Stuck with employment problems, health and safety or want advice on management training? This organisation provides links and forms to cover most of the eventualities you'll encounter together with more general business and economic news and features.

**Doing Business in**                              **www.claytonutz.com.**
**Australia**                                      **au/fr-bus.htm**
Useful booklet that provides foreign businesses with a clear guide to the legal, cultural and economic fundamentals of business life in Australia. Download and print out your own copy.

**Hints to Exporters**                             **www.brittrade.com/**
**Visiting New Zealand**                           **publications/new_zealand/**
The title says it all. It's an extraordinarily useful guide, packed with travel, business and etiquette tips that's up to date and essential reading for any business person off on travels. And there's a similar site for Australia at **www.brittrade.com/publications/australia/**

---

**Central and South America**

---

**AmchamNet**                                      **www.amcham.com.br**
Stacks of business information and advice on doing business in Brazil. Supplied by the American Chamber of Commerce, there's US bias, but it's a good briefing for any company.

**Argentina Business**                             **www.invertir.com**
A good place to start doing your homework if you're planning any trade in Argentina.

**Bankomext**            **http://mexico.**
**Business Centre**        **businessonline.gob.mx**
How to get started in Mexico, with good advice on economic and local labour plus details of local grants available and a directory of business contacts.

**Brazil Infonet**          **www.brazilinfo.net**
An introduction to the business side of Brazil, with local business and government contacts.

**BrazilBiz**          **www.brazilbiz.com.br**
Music to health products, banking to chemicals, this directory is loaded with business-to-business contacts in Brazil – just ignore the plentiful spelling mistakes.

**Camara Venezolano**        **www.britcham.**
**Britanica de Comercio (CVBC)**      **com.ve**
The British Chamber of Commerce provides a library of information that's a great place to start researching business methods and opportunities in Venezuela.

**ChileTrade.cl**          **www.chiletrade.cl**
What's on offer from Chilean companies – a database of import/export opportunities plus advice for foreign companies who'd like to invest in this east-coast strip of a country.

**Chile Business Directory**        **www.chilnet.cl**
A basic business Yellow Pages-style directory, but set apart by the import-export section of opportunities.

**Dominican Republic One**        **www.dr1.com**
Have a cigar – you've found one of the few sites covering basic details of business and economy in the Republic.

**Guatemala Online**        **www.quetzalnet.com**
Impressive directory and business advice combo that merges what's available on export with a guide to business.

**INEGI – National Institute of**        **www.inegi.**
**Statistics, Geography and Informatics**      **gob.mx**
How many and where they live – the numbers and statistics that define Mexico.

**Inter-American Development**        **http://database.**
**Bank Online Databases**        **iadb.org**
Thinking of tackling Latin America? Here's a good place to start: it's packed with details on trade, economy and social statistics on all the countries in the region. Or try the similar Latin American Network Information Centre (LANIC) site (**www.lanic.utexas.edu**).

**LatinFocus**        **www.latin-focus.com**
Great place for research into a Central or South American country. Pick your country from the list and view stacks of detailed data explaining the current economic situation.

**LatinInvestor**        **www.latininvestor.com**
Data, reports and advice (mostly in Spanish) geared to stock investors, but equally useful as background information for any business interested in the Central and South American markets.

**Peru Home Page**        **http://ekeko.rcp.net.pe**
Central portal to all sites Peruvian – including lots of net-stuff and business guides, such as the Central Reserve Bank of Peru (**www.bcrp.gob.pe**), that provide the latest in Peruvian high finance – and an overview of the local economic forecast.

---

**Europe**

---

**Albanian World Wide Web Home Page**      **www.albanian.com**
Tucked away above Greece, Albania's unlikely to be a major export market for many companies – but if you want to complete your European domination, here's country background, contacts and economic statistics to get you started.

**Athens Chamber of Commerce and Industry**    www.acci.gr
The official, and very good, government guide to doing business in Greece, together with a directory of links to other Greek trade and industry sites.

**Austrian Federal**                  www.wk.or.at/
**Economic Chamber**                  aw/aw_intl/
Background data promoting foreign trade with Austria. Or for a more officious view of the nation's finances, try the Bank of Austria (www.austria.eu.net/oenb/english)

**Belgian Federal**                  www.belgium.fgov.
**Government**                  be/en_index.htm
The state of political and economic play in Belgium.

**Belgium Business**                  www.infospace.com/uk.
**Finder**                  tetegr/intldb/bizfindint.htm?QO=BE
Hunt down a fine chocolate maker, or any other Belgian business with this specialist section of the giant Infospace search engine (and it's not just Belgians who get a spot – almost every other country has its own directory section).

**Bridge to Greece**                  www.greekvillage.com/
**and Cyprus**                  bridge/bridge.htm
An essential stop if you want to learn how to start trading in Greece or Cyprus. One of the best directories of local websites that provides financial, investment and import/export information.

**Britain in the European Union**    www.fco.gov.uk
Here's the Foreign Office policy (at least the official one) on Europe.

**British Chamber of Commerce in Germany**    www.bccg.de
The British view on trade in and with Germany – but with over 800 member companies, it's a powerful, and very useful, association that can provide basic or specialist advice together with a directory of local companies willing to trade.

**British Polish Chamber of Commerce**      **www.bccg.org.pl**
Need a lawyer in Warsaw or advice with marketing, shipping or accommodation? This non-profit organisation, like all Chambers of Commerce, is a great place to find out how to conduct business in a country. There's a British bias, but it's useful for anyone.

**British-Swedish**      **www.swednet.org.uk/**
**Chamber of Commerce**      **bscintro.html**
Looks dreadful, but if you want a directory of links to Swedish businesses, this is the best around – ideal if you want to find a partner company, local lawyer or bank. It also has concise reports on economic and business sectors.

**Business in Europe:**      **www.business-in-europe.**
**French Business Locations**      **com**
Still need persuading why you should relocate to St Tropez? All the information and advantages to doing business in France.

**Central and Eastern**      **www.ceebd.**
**European Business Directory (CEEBD)**      **co.uk**
Does almost exactly what the title suggests – a good reference point, but you'll need to visit another site, such as the British Council (www.britcoun.org) for background material and advice.

**Central Europe Online**      **www.invest.centraleurope.com**
News and market analysis and updates from the various countries in Central Europe. Subscribe to its daily email update, which delivers headlines and summaries to your in-box. Discussion groups provide a busy forum for natives and foreign investors to discuss the political and financial outlook.

**Central European Business Daily**      **www.cebd.co.uk**
Slick, impressive business news site reporting from Central Europe – and providing just about the best way to keep track of commerce in this part of the world.

**Chamber of Commerce and**        www.ccir.ro
**Industry for Romania and Bucharest**
Buy a bakery, stock up on surplus clothes or invest in local business opportunities – classifieds and advice to help you grow in the region together with a directory of Romanian companies on the web.

**Chamber of Commerce of the**        www.cc.lu
**Grand Duchy of Luxembourg**
A basic guide to the Luxembourg market for potential exporters, together with a modest directory of online industry.

**Confoederatio Helvetica**        www.admin.ch/ch/e/index.html
Want the official word from the Swiss government? Here's a simple directory to government departments within Switzerland that could help potential foreign business partners.

**Contact '99 –**        www.contactfinland.fi/
**Finland Business Services**        business.html
It's not just paper and mobile phones – an online directory of Finnish businesses.

**Council of Europe**        www.coe.fr
The organisation that promotes law and order and protects the member states.

**Croatian Chamber of Economy**        www.hgk.hr
The Balkans is not, perhaps, the most settled place to do business at the moment, but this site covers all aspects of trade and opportunities in impressive detail.

**Czech Info Centre**        www.muselik.com/czech/toc.html
Brew up a new relationship in the Czech market – wide range of concise guides and reports on the economy, doing business, travel, even a language course. And to help you find a business, there's a directory of companies online.

**Danish Exporters**        www.danish-exporters.tele.dk
This is the official government database of what's on offer in

Denmark. For a guide to local business and how best to form relationships with it, try the Danish Ministry of Business and Industry (www.em.dk/engvers.htm)

### Doing Business in Azerbaijan
www.soros.org/azerbjan/ azerbusi.html

Tough trading, perhaps, but there's still business and trade – here's the news and a modest range of guides to doing business from the Soros foundation; if you're interested in working with the smaller, less affluent central European countries, try the main Soros site (www.soros.org) for help, links, news and even grants.

### Economic Chamber of Macedonia
www.mchamber.org.mk

Confused by tricky import laws? A small market, but a good site with exports on offer and a good guide to the laws regulating foreign trade.

### Embassy of Italy in the United States
www.italyemb.org

Promoting Italy to the Americans with official (and sometimes officious) guides to business life in Italy, travel tips and a good directory of links to local Italian newspapers online – which provide all the current news and economic reports you could want.

### Romanian Embassy
www.roembus.org

Smart, useful business guides for anyone considering business in Romania.

### Estonian Ministry of Foreign Affairs
www.vm.ee

One of the richest countries among the Baltic States promotes its flourishing economy on this official site – but visit the Estonian Investment Agency if you'd prefer to do a deal with a local company and use ETA for the latest news.

### Euro Guide
www.euroguide.org

Essential directory to Euro-centric sites online.

### European Business Directory
www.europages.com

A great information portal that includes an impressive phone directory of companies in Europe, profiles and analysis of countries in Europe and a guide to doing business in Europe.

### Europa           www.europa.eu.int
Solid, worthy promotion of Euro-land with much talk of monetary union and central banks. If you're not European and want a basic grounding, it's a good place to start.

### France Business Protocol     www.worldbiz.com/bizfrance.html
Dealing with the French, it says here is a minefield of protocol. Do you need to wear a suit to meetings? And where do you turn if you've just relocated to Paris? And if you're doing business in Germany, visit sister site Germany Business Protocol (www.worldbiz.com/bizgermany.html).

### Francexport           www.francexport.com
Want to buy goods or services from a French company? Flick through the directory of services on offer and export opportunities from France.

### French Foreign Ministry       www.france.diplomatie.fr
International diplomacy – and the official line on trade with French companies.

### German Federal Ministry           www.
### for Foreign Affairs         auswaertiges-amt.de
Promoting German business and political relations with other countries.

### Go-Spain Business Pages      www.go-spain.com/business
Stacks of background briefings on Spanish business and industry, with particular emphasis on import and export opportunities.

### Greece Ministry of Foreign Affairs      www.mfa.gr
International trade – of goods and ideas – with Greek organisations.

### IDA Ireland           www.idaireland.com
Locate your base or your new factory in Ireland – the Industry Development Agency will help show you how.

**Interstate Statistical Committee** www.unece.org/
**of the Commonwealth of Independent States** stats/cisstat
What's the forecast for Uzbekistan or Moldova? The economic
state of the dozen countries that were part of the former Soviet
republic.

**Invest in Finland Bureau** www.investinfinland.fi
Enthusiastic reports on why you should locate your next base,
factory or shop in Finland – plus plenty of information on doing
business with the Finns.

**Invest in Sweden Agency** www.isa.se
Dry, official government words on how and why Sweden is great
for foreign companies.

**Ireland Government** www.irlgov.ie
Central access point to the Irish government's ministry of foreign
affairs, trade commission and source of local information.

**Irish Trade Web** www.itw.ie
Great place to start if you want to know how to do business in
Ireland, or with an Irish company. Doesn't stop there – also includes
trade shows and travel information. For a complete directory of
companies in Ireland, try the slick, bright Profiler section of Ireland
On-Line (http://home.iol.ie).

**Italian Chambers of Commerce** www.italchambers.net
Ideas for investment in Italy – plenty of classifieds offering business
opportunities. Or try the ItalTrade site that promotes international
trade with Italy; but make sure you visit Italy Business Protocol if
you want to avoid offending your potential partners.

**Italy Foreign Ministry** www.esteri.it/eng
Working to promote Italy and trade with international companies.

**Luxembourg** www.etat.lu
Central site for the smallest European country's official government
line on trade and policies.

**Netherlands Foreign Investment Agency**      **www.nfia.com**
Want to work with a Dutch company? Here's the official government site promoting exchange.

**Portugal Ministry of Finance**      **www.dgep.pt**
Portuguese economic forecasts and contacts for international trade.

**Sweden Finance Ministry**      **www.sb.gov.se**
Central government source for economic forecasts and international trade.

**Tenders Electronic Daily**      **http://ted.eur-op.eu.int**
Lists all the requests for tenders currently published by governments within the EU.

---

**Middle East**

---

**Arab Net**      **www.arab.net**
Unusual mix of pertinent business features – such as why foreign goods often do better than a local version, profiles of major corporations and economic digests of each country – and the silly, such as the A-Z of camels. Well worth a visit for one or the other.

**Central Bureau of**      **www.cbs.gov.il/**
**Statistics – Israel**      **engindex.htm**
The central repository for statistics about Israel's business, economy and culture.

**Dubai Internet Pages**      **http://dubai.uae-pages.com/business/**
Upbeat collection of useful and practical how-to business reports and executive summaries aimed at companies interested in trading with or investing in Dubai.

**Egypt Corporate**      **www.corporateinformation.com/**
**Information**      **egcorp.html**
The Egypt page from mammoth information provider Corporate Information; provides a great one-page summary of the main

corporate, political, financial and general news for Egypt, plus links to related databases listing all Egyptian companies and share prices.

### Iranian Trade Association                    www.iraniantrade.org

Tucked away in a corner of this non-profit US organisation is a good primer to doing business with Iran, but much of the rest promotes the idea of better relations between Iran and the USA.

### Israel Ministry of Foreign Affairs          www.israel.org/mfa

The Israeli government's view on its own country's political, economic, legal and cultural position. If you want a local business contact, try a specific directory such as the Israel Yellow Pages (www.yellowpages.co.il) that lists Israeli businesses.

### Lebanon.com                                  www.lebanon.com

Heady mix of Lebanese real estate companies, job banks and business agents vying for your attention – either as a local business seeking a new office or a foreign company ready to hire a new team.

---

## North America

---

### British-American Business Council (BABC)     www.babc.org

Common language, very different business cultures – the BABC sits in the middle to try to help make partnerships work.

### Business Broker Web                          www.business-broker.com

Want to retire gracefully? Sell your company through this broker – or expand your operations from the list on offer in the US and Canada.

### Canadian Commercial Corporation (CCC)        www.ccc.ca

The CCC helps smooth out any wrinkles for companies that want to import Canadian products.

## //HUMAN RESOURCES

Hiring and managing staff must rate as one of the most time-consuming jobs for any small business. It can take weeks to interview potential candidates for a job, then hours just filling in the correct forms required by the government.

To help part of the problem, you could use a recruitment agency. High-street agencies can easily charge 20-30% of the starting salary, simply to place someone who's already on their books. Internet-based agencies work in a similar way but usually charge far less. You will probably also get a wider range of applicants, due to the reach of the net. To help sort out the good from the bad, visit the psychometric testing sites to help you devise strategies to find hard-working dedicated staff.

Once you have staff, your business administration will start to revolve around them. Your accountant should be able to manage the payroll for you, and your bank can carry out a monthly direct transfer to their bank accounts – or you can outsource it to a specialist company.

Many small companies will have just a few staff and the entire process of hiring, training, managing and firing can be a very steep learning curve. Employing someone means paperwork – most of it from the government. As well as a basic contract, you'll have to sort out their national insurance, benefits, pension and tax. If you're a small company, you probably don't have a personnel department to do all this. Your accountant might be able to help with day-to-day stuff, but you will need forms. In the UK, the best place to go is the Institute of Personnel and Development (**www.ipd.co.uk**) or Law Pack publishing (**www.lawpack.co.uk**); in the USA, find your local State regulatory body through the WorkIndex directory (**www.workindex.com**).

## Starting points

**Institute of Personnel and Development**          **www.ipd.co.uk**
Official guides, advice, forms and plans to help you hire, manage and fire staff effectively.

**Training and Enterprise Councils**          **www.tec.co.uk**
Advice and information at a local level on the government's training and job schemes.

**TriNET VCO**          **www.trinetvco.com**
Don't waste time doing the payroll or managing your staff records – outsource it to these folk.

**WorkIndex**          **www.workindex.com**
Personnel problems or workplace safety, it's all covered in this impressive directory of sites.

## Workplace safety

**American Industrial Hygene Association**          **www.aiha.org**
Worried about safety, illness and hygiene in the workplace? This organisation cleans up in this area with regulations, policies and examinations.

**Hours of Labor**          **www4.law.cornell.edu/**
**and Safety**          **uscode/40/ch5.html**
It doesn't get much drier than this. The official US directives on working hours. Zzzz.

**Occupational Safety and Health**          **http://oshweb.me.tut.fi**
Impressive directory detailing just about every relevant site for workplace (and workers') safety.

**Worker Protection**          **www.usda.gov/**
**Standards**          **oce/oce/labor-affairs**
The official word – US legislation and directives that are in place to help protect workers.

## Testing and interviews

*Go for a job with an American company and you'll soon be run through a set of psychometric tests to check you're suitable material. In the UK and Australia, it's rather less scientific and still mostly based on a chat and maybe a test. If you're about to hire new staff and want to update your selection criteria, try these sites that have sample tests and the latest theories on spotting talent in the pool of potential human resource.*

**Assess Yourself Online**  www.srg.co.uk/assessyou.html
Try these tests to help spot a potential candidate's strengths (and weaknesses).

**Career Mapper**  www.ti.com/recruit/docs/resume.shtml
See how the mighty Texas Instruments filters initial candidates with its useful online form.

**Job Assessment**  www.namss.org.uk/jobassess.htm
Give it a go, have a psychometric test yourself online – also provides a directory of links to other useful sites.

**Mind Tools**  www.mindtools.com
Online tests that aren't specifically for jobs, but should spark ideas for tests of your own.

## Finding staff

**CareerCentral**  www.careercentral.com
Set up a profile for your ideal candidates and you'll get a list of matching jobseekers.

**CareerMosaic UK**  www.careermosaic-uk.co.uk
A database of vacancies sourced from a good selection of international companies, and you can search newsgroups for vacancies.

**CareerZine**   www.careerzine.co.uk
Over 5,000 jobs in the science, finance, admin and health fields.

**CreativeGroup**   www.creativegroup.com
Need a creative type? Stacks of ideas people and marketing staff
raring to go.

**e-job**   www.e-job.net/ejob.asp
Small, select range of jobs in advertising, marketing and sales.

**Gradunet-Virtual Careers Office**   www.gradunet.co.uk
Matches graduates to their perfect jobs.

**JobHunter**   www.jobhunter.co.uk
Gathers together jobs advertised in local newspapers – the
searchable database has over 21,000 job entries.

**Jobs Unlimited**   www.jobsunlimited.co.uk
Jobs in media, education and social areas that have been
advertised in the *Guardian* newspaper.

**JobSearch**   www.jobsearch.co.uk
Smart searches for your next job – submit your CV and your perfect
job description.

**JobSite UK**   www.jobsite.co.uk
Get a job in Paris or Petersham – scour the collection of over 7,000
jobs advertised by UK and European recruitment agencies; also
allows job-hunters to send a CV to the agencies.

**Jobworld**   www.jobworld.co.uk
The best choice of jobs for IT professionals – over 15,000 job
vacancies on offer.

**Reed Online**   www.reed.co.uk
Check out the salary you'll have to pay and get advice on hiring
from this high-street recruitment agency.

**Robert Half**   www.roberthalf.com
Need an accountant or financial director? Here's a stack of US,

European and Australian candidates from this specialist financial recruitment agency.

**Taps**                                                    **www.taps.com**

Thousands of IT, marketing, sales and finance jobs in Europe. The site's used to advertising jobs from hundreds of major UK and international companies, so is always busy.

### Unions and professional bodies

Almost every profession has an organisation at its heart that helps protect the members' interests – by negotiating decent pay or promoting a good code of conduct. And if you're about to close your main factory, you'll find a visit to the relevant trade association or union essential. For more information and advice, you'll find every union listed at **www.psr.keele.ac.uk/area/uk/tus.htm**.

## //NEWS

The net is the perfect medium for delivering news. Some sites store it in archives, so you can use it for research; others deliver it as it breaks, direct to your desktop or email inbox.

Best of all, you can choose what sort of your news you want – general, local, world, country-specific or industry-specific. If you're only interested in news about the automobile industry in France, or the computer industry in India, fine. You'll find both on world news websites and through custom email delivery services.

Almost all the news is free – with the exception of one or two financial investor sites that charge for tips and stock picks. You can browse the features from today's *Financial Times* as easily as the business reports – or cartoons – from the *Toronto Globe* and *Mail*. This provides one of the best features of the Internet – a global outlook on any event. If a story breaks in the USA, don't bother with summary tucked away on page seven of a British paper: visit the US sites and get all the details. To find a local paper for any country, visit a directory site such as NewsRack.

## Starting points

### CEO Express
www.ceoexpress.com

Supposedly designed for busy CEOs but actually useful for most business people who want a single-page index to almost every business paper, magazine and resource on the web – and you can customise it all to your requirements.

### InfoBeat
www.infobeat.com

Get your own daily newspaper delivered by email each morning – customise it to cover world news, weather, business, exchange rates or whatever. Free and simple.

## General news

*Most of the business megasites (see page 109) include the latest business news, as do niche business sites and portals such as Excite! and Yahoo! Here are some of the better news-only sites.*

### BBC News/Business    http://news.bbc.co.uk/hi/english/business/

Just about the best place to find news and reports (written, spoken and video) about world business, economies and the latest market information.

### NewsAlert
www.newsalert.com

Gathers together (mostly US) company news from a variety of sources to save you the effort.

### NewsRack
www.newsrack.com

Brilliant, simple idea done well – links to (almost) every online newspaper and magazine site from around the world. If it's not here, try the Paperboy at www.thepaperboy.com or Worldwide News at www.worldwidenews.com.

### Newswatch
www.newswatch.co.uk

Pulls out the business and financial stories from the UK press.

### Time
www.time.com

What's happening in the world, reviewed and analysed.

**ABC News**  www.abcnews.com/sections/business
US-centred news, but the depth and volume are very impressive.
Covers finance, market updates, business and even the odd event
outside the States.

**Advanced Financial Network**  www.advfn.com
Impressive UK financial and market news.

**AFX News**  www.afxnews.com
One of the best places for full coverage of international financial
news.

**CBS.MarketWatch**  http://cbs.marketwatch.com
Just about the best financial news site on offer, with excellent
coverage of breaking stories and market and company news,
together with tips, analysis and reports. All the usual excess of US
market information, but the European coverage beats
TheStreet.com.

**CNBC Europe**  www.cnbceurope.com
Over-designed site from the cable TV channel. Provides summaries
of business, finance and company news.

**CNNfn**  www.cnnfn.com
Vast, slick and very professional at the job of providing the latest
market and company news together with analysis and financial
features.

**DailyTish**  www.upside.com/DailyTish
The latest reports from Wall Street, with a welcome twist of
humour.

**Financial Times**  www.ft.com
Just about the best global view of the economic market.

**Fox Market Wire**  www.foxmarketwire.com
The web face of the cable news channel, with the usual news and
market reports. Unlike other sites, it includes some impressive live

video reports together with real-time price data for your fifty favourite stocks.

**MSNBC** www.msnbc.com
Multimedia-crazed financial news site packs in market news, reports, video segments, audio reports and jazzy graphics; best for new investors looking for carnival-style news presentation.

**The New York Times: business** www.nytimes.com/business
Full, free access to the stories from the business section of the day's paper and, as an added net-only bonus, there are also concise features on related background aspects of finances, such as law and education.

**Reuters MoneyNet** www.moneynet.com
International market and industry news from the global news experts. You can search the past month's news stories and, if you pay, get real-time share prices.

**TheStreet.com** www.thestreet.com
Huge collection of news, opinionated columns and articulate market reports team up with clever tools to help investors track shares, compare prices and dig out information for research. There's plenty of free information, but for commentary and the clever tools you'll need to subscribe.

**SiliconValley** www.siliconvalley.com
First stop for any high-tech VP looking for future eBay and Amazon.com-style successes. Polished site details news from the home of the US computer industry.

**UK Business Park** www.ukbusinesspark.co.uk
Gathers together the day's business and financial news and sends you a summary by email.

**Weekend City Press Review** www.news-review.co.uk
A summary of business and company news gathered from the main daily papers.

## Wall Street Journal                    www.wsj.com

For half the price of the printed edition, you can get the full text of each day's Journal for free – and get access to the archives of old stories.

## World coverage

### Agence France Presse              www.afp.com

Full coverage of world news in six languages (French, English, German, Spanish, Portuguese and Arabic) from a leading international press agency.

### Anorak                           www.anorak.co.uk

Originally sent to busy share-traders' screens to scan in their quiet moments, this site provides the quickest possible news fix. It condenses all the tabloid and broadsheet news and views into a mini commentary. Includes cartoons, showbiz, sport and great photos.

### CBS.MarketWatch           www.cbsmarketwatch.com

Yes, it's a US television slot, but its international news and features are just as good as any niche country-specific site.

### China Daily                      www.chinadaily.net

Essential reading for any company exporting to China or its provinces. English-language news from China, including local and world business, money and politics. For a general overview of how Chinese news impacts other countries, visit China News Digest (www.cnd.org).

### Crayon                           www.crayon.net

Create your own newspaper from the subject sections, features and cartoons available. If you want email delivery, try InfoBeat.

### The Christian Science Monitor      www.csmonitor.com

Not the religious rag you might expect, but a cool, balanced view on world news.

**Euromoney Online**            **www.emwl.com**

Impressive archive of current and past articles from the print magazine that reports on European markets – normally with a view to the global implications. You'll also find a good directory of links to European financial sites.

**Financial Times**            **www.ft.com**

The usual quality UK financial news and features you expect, but with good coverage of Africa, North and South America and the Middle East.

**InfoBeat**            **www.infobeat.com**

Get a custom-made daily paper delivered free via email. Not a unique service, but this is the best for world coverage.

**International Herald Tribune**            **www.iht.com**

World news, but without the glamour of CNN.

**Japan Press Network**            **www.jpn.co.jp**

High-powered but essential economic, financial and high-tech news from Japan.

**Kidon Media Link**            **www.kidon.com/media-link/**

Want to know what's happening in Uruguay or Slovenia? Links to over 6,000 country-specific news sites.

**The Nando Times**            **www.nando.net**

World news, regional US reports – and Dilbert – make up part of this nicely manageable rival to the big US news-busters.

**The New York Times**            **www.nytimes.com**

The world-view from Manhattan makes an impressive read. Everything from the paper plus the NY Review of Books and local guides to NY.

**NewsNow**            **www.newsnow.co.uk**

Gets you the news first. An impressive UK news service that provides world news updated every five minutes.

### NewsPage
www.newspage.com

World and business news on a grand scale – reports gathered from over 600 magazines and newspapers, then sorted into 2,500 topics. If it's out there, it's in here – but it can be rather overwhelming.

### Press Association
www.pa.press.net

Excellent coverage of news from around the world. Less US bias than CNN, and without the deluge provided by Reuters.

### Reuters
www.reuters.com

The biggest name in news-gathering from around the world includes a terrifying news ticker that rolls on relentlessly. Step off the home page and be overwhelmed by the quantity and quality of the subject-specific news.

### World News
www.wn.com

Fabulous portal gathering together world news from sources such as the *Jerusalem Post* and *South China Morning* Post. Best of all, it has vertical micro-sites covering specific business topics and industries.

---

### Business magazines online

---

*All the leading weekly and monthly business magazines have websites. The more enlightened, such as Business 2.0 and Forbes, publish the latest features and news on their sites. This benefits web addicts, who get the content for free, but they are also more likely to end up buying a copy next time they're away from a screen.*

### Accountancy Age
www.accountancyage.co.uk

News and features from the world of accounting from one of Britain's leading titles.

### Accountancy Magazine
www.accountancymagazine.com

Top-selling accountancy magazine provides features and news, together with an archive of stories covering ... well, accountancy.

**The Banker**                    www.thebanker.com
Features on the global changes in banking – and the impact of the
net rates as one of the most important issues for bankers.

**The Bankers' Almanac**          www.bankersalmanac.com
The bible for international banks.

**Banking and Technology**              www.btnsn.
**News Service Network**                     com
Keeping (mostly banking professionals) up to date with new
developments in the way money is moved and managed.

**BBC Online Business**   http://news.bbc.co.uk/hi/english/business
Vast archives and the latest business news – with text, sound and
video clips.

**Brill's Content**               www.brillscontent.com
Top features on the information and media age. Very sharp, very
readable, and an essential bookmark for anyone in the Internet or
media industry.

**Business 2.0**                   www.business2.com
The practical side of doing business with the new world order
defined by 'e'.

**Business Week Online**          www.businessweek.com
Free online version of the well-respected weekly provides features,
analysis and business trends, plus ratings for thousands of mutual
funds and specialist information archives on banking, travel and
careers for business people.

**The Economist**                  www.economist.com
Hugely influential economic and political analysis of global markets.
Publishes all its features online – and the Internet edition is free for
the first ten visits, but then you'll be charged a subscription.

**Fast Company**                   www.fastcompany.com
Cool, trendy high-tech magazine and similar companies and their
wannabes congregate to discuss.

**Forbes**                                          **www.forbes.com**
Impressive site that packs in all the current and past articles and
news stories together with new web-only features from this well-
respected business magazine – or just check who's worth what in
the famous league tables. Discussion groups let you chat about the
site's contents or business topics in general.

**Fortune**                                          **www.fortune.com**
Rather listless site mirroring the far better print version. Contains
company news, stories and interviews – together with its list of the
most dynamic companies in the US.

**Inc. Online**                                          **www.inc.com**
Just about the best magazine site for entrepreneurs and
enthusiastic business folk. Provides advice columns, discussion
forums and a vast directory of online resources.

**The Industry Standard**                       **www.thestandard.com**
The best reports, features and news about the Internet itself. The
metrics section is a brilliant résumé of what's up and down in this
virtual world.

**Marketing Week Online**              **www.marketing-week.co.uk**
Who's promoting what. All the content from the print edition, with
archive material and daily updates.

**Nikkei Net Interactive**                       **www.nni.nikkei.co.jp**
Trade with the East? Visit for a running list of the latest business
news headlines from Japan, together with company and market
news from the Tokyo stock exchange.

**Red Herring**                                    **www.redherring.com**
The business of technology – essential magazine reading for
anyone who wants to keep up to speed with the way new
companies are developing and using technology and re-defining
the business model.

## //REFERENCE AND RESEARCH

The sheer scale of information that's available on the Internet is enough to worry even the most dedicated librarian. There are dictionaries, encyclopaedias, company reports, government papers, business news archives, maps and gazetteers.

The reason that there's so much reference material around is historic – the Internet started life as an academic and education service; only recently has it opened up to the world of business. Apart from kids sorting out their homework, it's a great resource to help solve nagging questions about almost any aspect of business. You can look up the material yourself using any of the reference sites listed here, or ask one of the automated answer sites, such as AskJeeves or Information Please, which do their best to come up with a sensible answer.

The dangers? It's very easy to waste more time looking for something on the net rather than in a book, simply for the sake of using the net. And when you've found it, are you quite sure that the information is reliable and correct? By sticking to the big sites listed in this section, you can be reasonably certain that the information is true and accurate. Something that's no longer true if you stray off into other parts of the Internet.

### Starting points

**About.com**                                    **www.about.com**
A neat, wonderful place to start looking – a friendly community of experts, advice and features. Every topic has its own real human editor.

**Argus Clearinghouse**                        **www.clearinghouse.net**
Reference sites on the web, rated and categorised. Dull but ever so useful.

**CIA Worldbook**          **www.odci.gov/cia/publications/factbook/**
Slightly scary site (with a CIA page for kids and your tacit agree-

ment to be monitored) gives way to the impressively accurate Factbook with world statistics, maps and socio-economic info.

**refdesk.com**  **www.refdesk.com**
Check the weather, solve a crossword, do your sums – an impressive collection of links to tools and sites that'll help you out.

**Reference.com**  **www.reference.com**
Good haystack to start looking for your needle – lets you search newsgroups, mailing lists and websites in one fell swoop.

**Yahoo! Reference**  **http://dir.yahoo.com/reference**
The best reference sites from Yahoo!'s main catalogue.

---

**Dictionaries and encyclopaedias**

---

**A Web of On-line**  **www.facstaff.bucknell.edu/**
**Dictionaries**  **rbeard/diction.html**
Look up anything in any language; hundreds of bilingual and specialist English dictionaries – from Agriculture to Art, Hebrew to Hmong. Each comes from a different source, so the quality and bias cannot always be assured.

**AltaVista: Translations**  **http://babelfish.altavista.com**
Online translator to and from English and five other languages – type in your text or point it to a web page URL and choose the language combination. It's fast, and it actually works (kind of).

**Encarta**  **www.encarta.com**
Browse Microsoft's excellent Encarta encyclopaedia. Either search the free concise version (that's good enough for most searches) or subscribe to the deluxe edition – with a seven-day free trial.

**Encyclopedia.com**  **www.encyclopedia.com**
Free, concise encyclopaedia.

**Encyclopaedia Britannica**  **www.eb.com**
No longer in print but constantly updated material online. A free

trial lasts 30 days, then you pay a monthly $5 (about £3.50) subscription.

**Merriam Webster** www.m-w.com

Fine general US-English dictionary and thesaurus. Use A Web of Online Dictionaries for bilingual and specialist English words.

## Questions answered

**Ask an expert** www.askanexpert.com

Got a problem that's bugging you? These very clever people are waiting eagerly to answer your questions.

**AskJeeves** www.askjeeves.com

OK, it's really a search engine, but type in a question and it'll help you find the answer quickly.

**Information Please** www.infoplease.com

Easy reference to a vast combined resource of dictionaries, encyclopaedias, news archives and biographies.

**The Why Files** http://whyfiles.news.wisc.edu

Why o why o why o ... hang on, here's the answer. Patchy business help, but great for scientific and sports questions that have the office quiz team stumped.

**Xplore** www.xplore.com

Answers to nagging questions.

## Government information

**10 Downing Street** www.number-10.gov.uk

A potted summary of the Prime Minister's house and office – think of it as SOHO.

**Department of Commerce** www.doc.gov

US Government department responsible for exports, statistical data – oh, and the weather.

**Department of Labor**                    www.dol.gov
Helping Americans get ready for work – and manage their safety while there.

**Department of the Treasury**              www.ustreas.gov
Most businesses will know it as the place to file their taxes, but it also tries to manage a stable economy.

**Department of Trade and Industry (UK)**    www.dti.gov.uk
The British Government's organisation that promotes national and international business.

**Foreign Office**                        www.fco.gov.uk
The British stance on international business and affairs.

**Governments on the WWW**          www.gksoft.com/govt/
Stuck in Zaire or need a government official in Andorra? Government offices, banks, embassies and official state contacts for over 200 countries around the world.

**HM Treasury**                    www.hm-treasury.gov.uk
The UK's central government agency that sets interest rates, defines public spending and has overall control of the economy.

**Tagish's Directory of UK**              www.tagish.co.uk/
**Local Government Web Sites**        tagish/links/localgov.htm
Listing of every local government office in the UK and a link to the right website.

---

**Local information**

---

**County Web**                      www.countyweb.co.uk
UK-wide local directory for business, sports, attractions, towns and weather, arranged by county.

**DETR – Local Government**              www.local.doe.gov.uk
Responsible for the roads, environment and local government finances – though this site makes it hard to fathom this out.

## Scoot                     www.scoot.co.uk

Bookmark immediately. A brilliantly useful guide to everything you need in your local area. Derived from the Yellow Pages, it also provides local cinema listings and restaurant guides.

## Town Pages            www.townpages.co.uk

Find your local library, swimming pool and civic dump. There's a more comprehensive listings site at http://src.doc.ic.ac.uk/all-uk.html, but it's a little rough on design and navigation.

### Yellow Pages

*Everyone uses the Yellow Pages – now it's online and fully indexed; great for business-to-business or personal users who want to find a business.*

| | |
|---|---|
| **Australia** | **www.yellowpages.com.au** |
| **Canada** | **www.canadayellowpages.com** |
| **Ireland** | **www.nci.ie/yellow/** |
| **New Zealand** | **www.yellowpages.co.nz** |
| **South Africa** | **www.easyinfo.co.za** |
| **UK** | **www.yell.co.uk** |
| **USA** | **www.bigyellow.com** |

### Company research

*In the UK, companies file annual reports detailing accounts, profit and turnover with Companies House (www.companies-house.gov.uk). You can get a copy of these accounts for a fee, or use a company such as Dun and Bradstreet (www.dunandbrad.co.uk) to provide (for a fee) a credit or trading report on the company. In the USA, the equivalent is EDGAR – a method of submitting companies' reports in electronic form. These are more comprehensive and also cover public offers and bankruptcy – and, best of all, you can get them free.*

**Companies Online**                     www.companiesonline.com
Combined effort from Lycos and Dun and Bradstreet to help you find the home site for a company you're researching.

**Company Sleuth**                       www.companysleuth.com
Scours the web and news sources to gather together information and news about publicly traded companies – then sends you an email with its results.

**Dialog**                               www.dialog.com
Astonishing depth of information thanks to the merger of MAID and Knight-Ridder's company information services. Just about all the business, legal, corporate and company news you could want.

**Dun and Bradstreet**                   www.dunandbrad.co.uk
One of the best-known providers of company reports and credit ratings. Run a check before you open an account for an unknown company, or use them to help get money from unpaid invoices.

**Federal Filings Online**               www.fedfil.com
Hunt out every type of document filed with the US federal government – from bankruptcy notices through to IPOs and court cases.

**Free Edgar**                           www.freeedgar.com
Simple search tool that retrieves the very latest news and company documents from US companies. Most other sites provide only delayed access – or charge.

**Hoover's Online**                      www.hoovers.com
Vast, detailed and very knowledgeable company reports, news, analysis, forecasts and industry indicators form the basis of this well-known database. You can search the lot for a monthly fee.

**WhoWhere? Edgar**          www.whowhere.lycos.com/Edgar/
Search the archive of SEC documents or set up an email alert to tell you when a particular company files a new document.

## //SALES AND MARKETING

With a potential audience of hundreds of millions of users, the web is a fast, efficient, cheap, inventive and fun way to market your products to new customers. You can cut the cost of direct mail using electronic mail, drop advertising in glossy magazines in favour of banner ads or simply improve press relations.

Marketing on the Internet is not without its problems and pitfalls. All these are covered in detail in Chapter 5. In this section, we cover the ways in which you can use the net to change your traditional marketing – from buying balloons to hiring a guest speaker for a product launch.

Perhaps the obvious way to reach the new global audience is to send out a million emails to unsuspecting users promoting your new widget – don't. You'll get flamed with hate mail and damage your company's reputation. Read the section of dos and don'ts on page 98, and only use get a list from one of the reputable suppliers. You'll also find good advice on many business megasites (page 109) and from trade organisations such as the DMA (**www.the-dma.com**).

---

### Starting points

**Advertising Association**                **www.adassoc.org.uk**
Does its best to regulate the advertising trade within the UK.

**American Marketing Association**                **www.ama.org**
Help and advice for anyone using or involved in marketing.

**American Small**                **www.salesdoctors.com/**
**Business Association**                **directory**
Wondering how to promote a widget? Read over a thousand articles on marketing and publicity, provided by the ASBA.

**DoubleClick**                **www.doubleclick.net**
One of the biggest web companies that no one knows about. They

look after the majority of the banner advertising you see on websites; they buy space, sell ads, audit and provide PR.

### Guerrilla Marketing Online                     www.gmarketing.com
Tough tactics to help get results online.

### More Business                                  www.morebusiness.com
Heaps of good advice and features that show how to make the most of your business, particularly through use of marketing and advertising.

### Wilson Internet Services                       www.wilsonweb.com
Yes, Ralph's a consultant, but the site is a gem. It includes his well-written newsletters on just about every aspect of Internet commerce and marketing. If you're planning a business website or an update, visit and read good advice.

---

### Direct mail and email

---

### Alphasoft Net.Mailer                           www.alphasoftware.com
Clever software that's far more efficient than your email program for bulk mailshots.

### Arial Software Campaign                         www.arialsoftware.com
Software to help you manage your email list and post off the thousands of messages.

### Colorado Soft WorldMerge                        www.coloradosoft.com
Custom software that'll mail merge email address lists for a speedy way to send bulk mail.

### Direct Email List Source                        www.copywriter.com/lists/
Want to reach golfers or business people? Here's a list of lists for rent. Thousands of lists and resources provide a good place to start hunting.

### Direct Email Marketing                          www.e-target.com
Hundreds of targeted opt-in email address lists to help you sell more stuff.

**Direct Marketing Association**                    www.the-dma.com
Masses of good advice, and a code of conduct, to help prevent you
blundering around upsetting people.

**Direct Marketing News**                    www.dmnews.com
Stacks of information about how to write, design and target direct
mail, then send it by email or old-fashioned postal service. Plus
news, jobs and a great daily email newsletter that'll keep you up to
speed on the industry.

**Direct Marketing Club of Southern California**    www.dmcsc.com
Just one of dozens of local clubs online – its discussion group is a
good place to ask basic questions you wouldn't dare talk about in
a bigger national group. Or just read the advice on creating a piece
and maintaining privacy.

**ELetter**                    www.eletter.com
Here's a cool way to tie together the net and traditional postal
services. Visit the site, upload (send them) your mailing list of
addresses and a document with your advertising piece, pay up
and go. The company prints the letter, catalogue or flyer, folds and
collates, then mails them out to the contacts. A great way for
international companies to test out the US market.

**Everything E-mail**                    www.everythingemail.net
As you'd guess, everything from software to advice, resources and
lists for rent.

**infoUSA**                    www.infousa.com
Target your mailshot; use this vast database of the addresses of
hundreds of millions of Americans sorted by area, type or interests.

**Interact**                    www.interact.com
If you use the top-selling ACT! contact database, here's a way to
integrate and share the information with colleagues – via the web.

**MailKing**                    www.mailking.com
Keeps you sane when managing bulk mailings.

### Mailing-Labels                    www.mailing-labels.com
A vast database of traditional mailing contacts in the UK that can
be defined by categories, interests or regions – then pay, download
the list and wait for the response. Rival company ListsNow
(www.listsnow.com/uk/) offers a similar service but is not as easy
to use.

### Stamps.com                           www.stamps.com
Buy postage credits, then use the special software to (legally) print
US stamps directly from your computer. Great for SOHOs that don't
want a franking machine.

### Yahoo!                                 www.yahoo.com
Yahoo's directory is a good place to start looking for lists, software
and ideas.

---

## Exhibitions and conventions

---

### Association for                          www.martex.
### Conferences and Exhibits                 co.uk/ace/
Great directory of organisers, designers, suppliers and specialists
who can help you put together the perfect conference or slick
visuals and a stand for your next show.

### Celebrity Speakers International      www.speakers.co.uk
If you fancy a pop celeb or notable political figure to open or talk at
your event, here's where to find them. Alternatively, try Now You're
Talking (www.nyt.co.uk).

### Exhibit Connections          www.exhibit-connections.com
Don't stress out – leave it to someone else to design, erect and
manage your next trade show stand.

### Exhibitions and Displays Direct  www.exhibitions-displays.co.uk
Rent or buy a small, modest display or a vast, shiny stand for your
next show.

### Exhibitions round the world       www.exhibitions-world.com
Cars, books, fashion: they all have trade shows – here's a mam-

moth calendar of over 4,000 conventions and exhibitions that happen around the world.

**Expobase** www.expobase.com

Vast multilingual, multi-country database of business trade shows together with suppliers that cover accommodation, travel and stand design and production.

**ExpoWeb** www.expoweb.com

When and where you'll find just about any show that's related to medical, food, computing and gaming industries.

**Trade Show Exhibits** www.tradegroup.com

Commission a super stand for your next trade show from this specialist design company.

**Venue Directory** www.venuedirectory.com

From hotels to stadiums, you'll find the perfect UK venue for your next event somewhere in here.

**Yahoo!** http://uk.dir.yahoo.com/
**Conventions** Business_and_Economy/Companies/
**and Trade Shows** Conventions_and_Trade_Shows/

Stacks of links to show organisers, designers and event managers – from the Yahoo! directory.

---

**Promotional materials**

---

**Accolade** www.accolade.uk.com

Good with big, personalised products including coffee machines, radios and cameras – as well as the usual watches and bags.

**B-loony** www.b-loony.co.uk

Want someplace that makes balloons? You've found it.

**Castelli Diaries** www.castelli.co.uk

Keep your logo relevant through the year with smart promotional diaries and appointment books.

**Mousemats**                                 www.mousemats-r-us.com

Get your message across to computer users – with your own mousemat or wrist-rest.

**Promotional**                               www.netcomuk.co.uk/
**World**                                     ~pukka/promotion.html

Plastic signs for your vans, shop or show.

**Salesbuilders**                             www.salesbuilders.co.uk

One of the widest ranges of promotional stuff around – from plastic folders to food and wine.

**Stress Relievers**                          www.stress-relievers.com

Makers of those squeezie beanbag things aimed at stressed out execs.

**Yahoo!**                                    http://uk.dir.yahoo.com/
**Promotional**                    Business_and_Economy/Companies/
**Items**                             Marketing_and_Advertising/
                                      Advertising/Promotional_Items/

If you want promotional stuff, there are thousands of sites offering every type of gizmo in here – almost too many.

### Advertising agencies

*Ad agencies will create a new campaign, re-design your brand or simply book national advertising space. If you want to use banner ads (the little oblong adverts that litter most commercial websites), see page 66. None of the major ad agencies have websites that do anything except promote their brand and range of services. If you want to know more, you'll need to call and arrange a meeting. Here are some of the best-known names.*

**Abbott Mead Vickers**                       www.amvbbdo.co.uk
**Bartle Bogle Hegarty**                      www.bbh.co.uk
**BMP DDB**                                    www.bmp.co.uk
**DMBB**                                       www.dmbb.com
**Grey**                                       www.grey.co.uk

| | |
|---|---|
| J Walter Thompson | www.jwtworld.com |
| Leo Burnett | www.leoburnett.com |
| Lowe Howard Spink | www.lowehoward-spink.co.uk |
| McCann Erickson | www.mccann.com |
| Saatchi & Saatchi | wwww.saatchi-saatchi.com |
| Young & Rubicam | www.yandr.com |

## //TRAVEL

Cut-price tickets, instant confirmation and more maps and guides than you will ever need fill this section. High-street travel agents have never been under such a threat, with some online booking agents prepared to lose money on ticket sales in their battle to win customers.

Online travel agents can often beat your local shop thanks to near-zero overheads and an automated service that's usually, but not always, fast and accurate. Most online travel agents are aimed at the consumer – the notable exception is BizTravel. However, they can all get cheap bucket-shop deals (if you're starting out in business) and business-class deals (if you're executive material). And if you've really hit the jackpot, try NetJets for a slice of your own jet.

Online travel agents let you plan complex journeys, book flights, hotels and car hire with just a few clicks. And some of the travel sites even remember your preference of seat, choice of meal and style of hotel to ensure that you'll get exactly what you expect. To help make up for the hours spent travelling, make sure you're signed up with a frequent flyer programme – and that the online travel agent does its best to maximise the points at the lowest cost. You can always trade in your points for a holiday – when you finally get some time off.

To try to claw back direct ticket sales, many airlines have spent a lot of effort improving their sites and now offer specific seat allocation (not normally available through a travel agent) or regular auctions of cut-price tickets. At the moment these are normally restricted to short-notice flights; once you've registered, you'll be sent an email whenever there's a special deal available. Try the big US carriers such as United (www.ual.com) or American (www.american.com).

To help you get to your destination, use one of the online maps that can print out precise instructions for driving or walking between appointments; and look at the destination guides for things to see and places to eat when you're not stuck in meetings. To make sure that you don't offend your new business contacts, visit the specialist sites offering language guides and advice on business etiquette.

## Airlines

*All the main airlines have their own sites. Most let you buy tickets online, check timetables and look at seating plans to make sure you're not next to the toilet. If nothing else, you can join their frequent flier schemes and check on your progression up to gold level.*

| | |
|---|---|
| **Aer Lingus** | **www.aerlingus.ie** |
| **Aeroflot** | **www.aeroflot.org** |
| **Air Canada** | **www.aircanada.ca** |
| **Air France** | **www.airfrance.com** |
| **Alitalia** | **www.italiatour.com** |
| **American** | **www.americanair.com** |
| **British Airways** | **www.british-airways.com** |
| **British Midland** | **www.iflybritishmidland.com** |
| **Cathay Pacific:** | **www.cathaypacific.com** |
| **Continental** | **www.flycontinetal.com** |
| **Delta** | **www.delta-air.com** |
| **EasyJet** | **www.easyjet.co.uk** |
| **El Al** | **www.elal.co.il** |

| | |
|---|---|
| Go | www.go-fly.com |
| Iberia | www.iberia.com |
| KLM | www.klmuk.com |
| Lufthansa | www.lufthansa.co.uk |
| Olympic | www.olympic-airways.gr |
| Qantas | wwww.qantas.com |
| Ryanair | www.ryanair.ie |
| SAS | www.sas.se |
| Singapore Airlines | www.singaporeair.com |
| TWA | www.twa.com |
| United | www.ual.co.uk |
| Varig | www.varig.com.br |
| Virgin | www.fly.virgin.com |

## Starting points

**Airlines of the World**  www.flyaow.com
Need to check a schedule or seat configuration? Find any airline's
website here.

**Fit for Business**  www.fitforbusiness.com
Not a dreaded financial check-up, but a friendly welcome for gung-
ho execs with boundless energy who want to swim, jog or work
out at every hotel they visit.

**The EmbassyWeb**  www.embpage.org
Your local embassy – whatever your nationality, wherever you are.

**How Far Is It?**  www.indo.com/distance/
This site will tell you the distance between any two towns or cities
in the world and, for towns in the same country, you'll also get
driving instructions and a map. Brilliant.

**Placeware**  www.placeware.com
Here's a novel idea. Don't travel – instead, book an online meeting
room and send out email invitations to the people you want to see.
You won't rack up the frequent flier points, but it's a lot cheaper.

### Roadnews.com
www.roadnews.com

You've landed in LA, your laptop's at the ready and you realise you've forgotten the adapter to connect your modem to the phone. This site helps out with news, tips and supplier listings for batteries, connectors and more. Trouble is, if you cannot connect to the web, how do you access the site?

## Travel agents

### A2bTravel
www.a2btravel.com

Vying for top slot as best UK travel agent site. Everything your local agent can provide and so very much more. Also worth checking prices at the websites of real agents FlightBookers (www.ebookers.com) and Trailfinders (www.trailfinders.co.uk).

### BizTravel.com
www.biztravel.com

Totally geared to business travellers (though generally American ones). You can organise your entire trip – from flights to car rental – on this site. Best feature? It'll automatically maximise your frequent flyer points and make the most of your expense account trips. Great for business users, but not always the cheapest tickets.

### HotelWorld
www.hotelworld.com

Find a hotel before you arrive, then book it online. Thousands of hotels in hundreds of countries.

### Leisure Planet
www.leisureplanet.com

See the hotel before you book; a vast collection of over 50,000 hotels each with a mini slide show plus area guides.

### MSN Expedia
www.expedia.msn.co.uk

Microsoft lands in the UK. Everything you need to research destinations and book flights, hotels and cars instantly. Good design with piles of information.

### Eurostar
www.eurostar.com

Travel to France and Belgium made very easy.

**NetJets** www.netjets.com

Feeling flash? Forget the travel agent and switch to fractional jet ownership, where every millionaire can own a bit of a Lear jet. Similar service from FlexJet (www.flexjet.com) – or buy a complete plane at LearJet (www.learjet.com).

**Travelocity** www.travelocity.co.uk

Just about the biggest travel agent on the web. Gives you instant access to the same system that's used by the high-street travel agents.

## Frequent flier schemes

**AirBank** www.airawards.com

Cash in your frequent flyer points – literally – by selling them here for dollars.

**FrequentFlier** http://frequentflier.com

Keep up to date with frequent flyer schemes.

**WebFlyer** www.webflyer.com

Choose your frequent flyer scheme with care, advises Randy. He'll tell you why and plenty more besides.

## Guides and maps

**CIA Worldbook** www.odci.gov/cia/publications/factbook/

Slightly scary site (with a CIA page for kids and your tacit agreement to be monitored) gives way to the impressively accurate Factbook with world statistics, maps and socio-economic info.

**City Net** www.city.net

What's going on in cities around the world – aimed at travellers but great for research or homework. Includes local transport, restaurants, guidebooks, accommodation, sights and customs.

**Lonely Planet** www.lonelyplanet.co.uk

Fantastic guidebooks to almost every world destination; best for experienced travellers eager to get as much as possible from their trip.

### MapQuest                                    www.mapquest.com
Search for a place, then plot a map – in extraordinary street-level detail – for the world.

### Maps Worldwide                              www.mapsworldwide.co.uk
Find your way around any city or country

### MultiMap                                    www.multimap.com
Got a UK phone number? Type it in and get a map of the local area. A neat add-on to the site's core business of providing street-level maps of the UK.

### The Original Tipping Page                   www.tipping.org
How, when and what to tip. Aimed at visitors to the US, but helps out around the world.

### Railtrack                                   www.railtrack.co.uk
Clean, simple, efficient – and it works. Much better than nagging National Rail Enquiries, but you should probably do that too.

### Rough Guides                                www.roughguides.com
Great guides to countries and cities for independent travellers on tight budgets.

### Travelang                                   www.travlang.com
Phrases to help you out when you're travelling.

### Travel Etiquette                            www.traveletiquette.com
Before you leave on a business trip, visit this site to make sure that you don't do something that will offend, be misinterpreted or amuse your business hosts.

### UK Street Map                               www.streetmap.co.uk
Whip out your laptop, link to your cell phone, and generate a map centred on any postcode or London street name. Alternatively, look it up in the A-Z, or ask a passer-by.

# 10//FAQS – FREQUENTLY ASKED QUESTIONS

As you start to use the Internet you're bound to come across questions, worries and problems. Many of these are dealt with in the relevant chapter in the main part of this book; for example, if you want to know how to find a credit reference for a potential customer, look to page 47.

However, you're bound to have a long list of niggles and worries that you're just not sure about. In this section, we've covered the most commonly asked questions and their answers.

## //WEBSITES

**Q How do I get started with this website stuff?**
**A** First, register a domain name that's representative of your company or its products (see page 25). If you want a very simple site, you could design it yourself – or ask your design department to help – using a word processor or simple web design program. For more complex sites with a database or snazzy graphics, it's probably more efficient to hire a specialist production company. To actually publish your site, you'll need to pay to rent disk space from a website provider or, if it's a big site, install your own server in the office (but this is very complex).

**Q It all sounds very complicated – I just want to sell my goods online. How do I do that?**
**A** One of the simplest ways of setting up an online catalogue is to use an all-in-one service (there's one on offer from VirginBiz, www. virginbiz.net) that helps you design the pages, enter the information and will even process credit card sales for you – with little specialist knowledge and no extra software needed on your part.

**Q If I publish a website, can anyone copy the information?**
**A** Broadly speaking, yes. If you have copyright information, make

sure that you add a copyright notice to the bottom of each page – it won't stop anyone, but it'll help you prosecute. To cut down on copying, you could format the information into small sections that can only be displayed one at a time (for example, displaying one entry of an encyclopaedia at a time), or you could ask users to register (and perhaps pay) before using the material. However, except for a few highly advanced tricks, anything that's displayed on a web page can be printed or copied.

*Q* **I want to set up a secure website to accept payments – what do I need?**
*A* You will need to talk to your website provider who can install the SSL (Secure Sockets Layer) feature you need to operate a secure website. Once you have this, any information a user types in is protected from hackers. Online payments normally means credit card payments – to accept these, you'll need to sign a contract with a card authorisation bureau that can check the card number in a second and manage the process of debiting the card account and crediting your account. See page 47 for more details.

*Q* **Can I stop people changing what's on my website?**
*A* Hackers love trying to change the content of the big websites (such as Microsoft's), but they rarely bother with smaller sites. Ask your website provider how they have implemented security – normally, you'll need a password and user ID to access the computer where your website files are stored. Don't forget to protect the software you use to design the website in your office, or a malicious employee will be able to wander over and change the wording of the website.

## //SECURITY

*Q* **What's a secure connection?**
*A* Secure connections are set up by the web server (not by your web browser) – you can tell you've got a secure connection when the tiny closed padlock icon is displayed at the bottom of the screen.

**Q Why can't I read my bank account details from the office?**
**A** Most office networks connect to the Internet via a firewall – a device that stops hackers getting into your office computers. Trouble is, many of these won't allow access to secure websites. And, besides, many companies don't like it if employees use the net for personal reasons during company time.

**Q Can anyone else read the emails I send?**
**A** Email messages are sent in plain text form – as you typed it out. As the email passes across the Internet, malicious system managers could, in theory, read it. However, with hundreds of millions of mail messages zipping around the net every day, it's unlikely. If you want to make quite sure that the head of IT in the company isn't peeking at private post, scramble the contents of your messages. The most secure system around is called PGP (www.pgp.com), although most email programs have some form of encryption built in.

**Q Hang on: doesn't storing passwords help me, rather than cause a security hole?**
**A** Your browser can save your password and user name and store these in a file together with the address of the page they refer to. Next time you log in, your browser can fill in your details for you. This is great, but don't forget it'll let anyone else who's using your computer gain full access to your account. In fact, the chances are that the bank and other sensitive sites you want to access will automatically turn off this feature. To make quite sure, choose the Tools/Internet Options menu and select the security tab. Now choose the Maximum setting and you'll be pretty safe.

**Q Should I be worried about cookies?**
**A** No, they are normally perfectly harmless. Most big sites use a cookie (it's a little file on your hard disk that lets a website store information on your machine) to store your name or preferences or the last time that you visited the site. Many shops and banks use cookies on your computer to keep track of who you are or what's in your shopping cart (trolley). If you turn off this feature, you might cut off access to these sites.

# //BROWSING

**Q** I have downloaded a nifty share-price program that ends in the ZIP extension. When I double click to run it, nothing happens. Why?

**A** A ZIP file contains a compressed version of the original file(s), squeezed down to save space and time when downloading. To unzip your file, you'll need an unzip program. The best known is WinZip from www.winzip.com.

**Q** Why does my web browser keep crashing?

**A** It shouldn't. This probably means that you're not using the latest version of the browser. As new ways of enhancing web pages are developed, older browsers can find it hard to manage and simply stop working. Visit www.microsoft.com or www.netscape.com to download the latest version of your browser.

**Q** Why isn't a website there any more?

**A** The website may have been closed down or, more likely, the designer has redesigned the site and reorganised the way the pages are stored and given them new names. If a page doesn't work, visit the main site's home page.

**Q** What does 'Error 404 not found' mean?

A It means that the address of a web page does not exist. Either you typed in the wrong address or the site has been redesigned and the names of the web pages have been changed.

**Q** Do all web page addresses start with the letters 'www'?

**A** No. You'll often see addresses that look very odd but will still work fine. The way addresses are created is slowly changing, so you can expect to see more addresses that are just names.

**Q** I saved some images from a website to my hard disk. Now how can I view these GIF and JPEG format files on my PC?

**A** The simplest method is to use your web browser as the viewer. Start your browser (choose not to connect and to work offline); start Windows Explorer. Click and drag one of the images from

Explorer on to the browser and you'll see it displayed. The alternative is to use a paint program that's better than Paint, installed with Windows. Try Paintshop Pro (www.jasc.com) or search www.filez.com for a wide selection.

**Q What's a plug-in?**

**A** A plug-in is a special bit of software that adds a new feature to your web browser. For example, if you want to view video or animation in your browser, it needs to have a plug-in that supports this. If you visit a site that uses snazzy multimedia tricks and you don't have the right plug-in, you'll be told and given the chance to download the file required.

**Q I want to use Bitmap images I created on my PC on my own web page. How can I do this?**

**A** You can, generally, use only GIF and JPEG format graphics files on a web page. You'll need to use an image editor program to convert your BMP format files to either GIF or JPEG. Try Paintshop Pro (www.jasc.com) or search www.filez.com.

**Q I've been told to clean out my cache – why?**

**A** Your cache (pronounced 'cash') is a folder where your web browser temporarily stores the images and text files for the web page it's visiting. Most web browsers set aside tens of megabytes of hard disk space for the cache so that they can store thousands of web pages. The advantage is that next time you visit the page, the browser will pull up the files from your hard disk rather than from the slow web link. If your browser seems to run very slowly, your cache may be too big or too full. Choose the Options/Network Preferences menu in Netscape or go to Tools/Internet Options/General and click on the Settings button in IE. You can now adjust the size of your cache (don't make it any bigger than 15-20Mb) or clear it.

**Q When I try to save a page with the File/Save As option in my browser, it just saves the text and layout – not the graphics. Why?**

*A* You need to use an offline browser that will grab all the associated files and store them on your hard disk. Try WebWhacker (www.webwhacker.com).

*Q* **When I visit some of the cool sites, my browser tells me I need to download a plug-in. Why, if I click Cancel, is the page is still displayed?**
*A* The cool sites you visit probably use animation, sound or video clips in their web design. If your browser cannot support these effects, it tells you and tries to download the appropriate plug-in (a little program that upgrades your browser). If you don't download the plug-in, the website will still work fine, but you'll not see the snazzy multimedia effects.

*Q* **I download lots of files from the Internet. I always check these with my virus scanner before I run the program, but what do I do with a compressed ZIP file?**
*A* When you unzip the contents of a ZIP file, it won't start any virus that's present; this means you can safely unzip the files and then run your normal virus scanner on the resulting files. However, if you're nervous about doing even this, you can ask the splendid WinZip utility (www.winzip.com) to scan the contents of a ZIP file before you open it up. Choose the Options/Program Locations menu in WinZip and enter the name of your virus-scanning software. Now you can scan ZIP files from the Actions menu.

*Q* **How can I be sure to download a file as quickly as possible?**
*A* If you are downloading a file from a commercial site, such as CNET, you'll be given a list of various sites that store this file. You could choose the nearest geographic site, but use lateral thinking and pick a site in the world where it's still night-time – the traffic will be much lighter and your download should fly.

*Q* **Can I catch a virus by looking at a web page?**
*A* Viewing images, entering information in a form or just viewing text on a web page is perfectly harmless. That means 99% of all

websites are fine. Sometimes, you'll visit a website that uses snazzy multimedia or other trickery. You may be warned that your web browser needs to download a plug-in or Java or ActiveX applet (the name for a little program). These applets are normally developed to provide extra functions – such as shopping carts, multimedia or special effects. However, it is possible to write nasty little applets that trash the files on your computer. To avoid this, don't accept plug-in downloads from sites where you don't know the company.

**Q Can I stop my staff viewing porn online?**
**A** Yes, almost totally. Use one of the control programs described in Chapter 2.

## //DISCUSSION, EMAIL AND CHAT

**Q I have been offered a mailing list with millions of email addresses on it. Should I send them all news of my new wonder product?**
**A** No. It's called spamming and it's horrible. It's also killing the net by slowing everything down. Lastly, you'll be thrown off your ISP and your company name will be mud. That should be pretty clear!

**Q I gave out my email address in a newsgroup – now I'm getting junk mail. Is there anything I can do?**
**A** Unsolicited junk mail – called spam – is the bane of life with email. Foolish companies send out millions of messages and think it'll improve their image. Many ISPs now have anti-spam systems in place that automatically recognise known culprits and reject any mail received from them. You don't have to do anything – but check with your ISP to see if they have this feature. Alternatively, if you keep getting junk mail from a particular address, you can create a new filter (or rule) in your email program that automatically deletes any message from this person as soon as it's received.

*Q* **I've joined a business mailing list but now I want to get off. Unfortunately, I've deleted the original instructions that tell me how to unsubscribe from the list. What can I do?**
*A* Visit the www.liszt.com site and search for your list. Under the description, it should give you instructions about how to subscribe and unsubscribe to the list. If not, see if there is an admin email contact and send them an email.

*Q* **How can I search for old newsgroup messages?**
*A* You need to use one of the archive sites – such as Deja (**www. deja.com**) – that store copies of messages from all newsgroups.

*Q* **Can I write a test message before diving in?**
*A* Yes, use the alt.test newsgroup – don't write test messages to a normal newsgroup or you'll get a lot of rude replies.

*Q* **How do I find a website that has a discussion forum?**
*A* The best place to look is ForumOne – **www.forumone.com**. It's not comprehensive, but it's about the best there is.

# //GLOSSARY

The Internet is packed with as many bewildering jargon terms, acronyms and other types of abbreviation as programmers can invent. To help you understand what's going on, here's a guide to the terms you'll encounter as you explore the net.

**access log** A file on your website server (created and set up by your ISP) that contains a record of every visitor to your website, when they visited and which pages they viewed – feed this into an access log analyser program and you'll get reports on your most popular pages and products. Essential to monitor response to your website and ad campaigns.

**access provider** See ISP.

**address** (email) The unique name that identifies a person and lets you send them a mail message. Written in the form 'simon@virginbooks.com'.

**address** (website) The unique location of a site on the web. Sometimes called a URL (Uniform Resource Locator).

**address book** A list of names and their email address. Your email program provides this feature to let you manage your contacts.

**ADSL Asymmetric Digital Subscriber Lines.** New system of transferring information over a standard telephone cable at very high speeds – several thousand times faster than a modem.

**anti-virus program** Special software that detects and removes viruses from programs and documents. You should run an anti-virus program on any file you download from the Internet or receive via email.

**applet** A small program that's downloaded from a website and runs within your web browser. Some online shops implement their shopping cart system using an applet.

**attachment** A file sent with an email message.

**authentication** Unique electronic certificate issued to a company so that they can prove that they are who they claim to be. The certificates (issued by independent companies such as VeriSign at **www.verisign.com** and Thawte at www.thawte.com) are used as part of an SSL (secure sockets layer) link on a secure server.

**banner ad** The small, rectangular-shaped advertisements that litter almost every commercial website on the net. They advertise some product or service and try to entice you to click on them – to view the original site. If you're a surfer, they are a nuisance; if you run a commercial site, they provide good income; if you are an advertiser, they offer a way of reaching a highly targeted audience. See also click through and impression.

**bit** A basic storage unit used in computers; a bit can only be one of two values, '1' or '0'. Data is stored in a computer as a combination of bits (eight together are referred to as a byte). Bits are normally used when specifying the transmission speed of a modem (for example, 56Kbps means 56,000 bits sent every second).

**bookmark** A way of storing the address of an interesting website in your web browser. When you want to revisit the site, don't bother typing in the address: just click on the bookmark entry. Microsoft and AOL call this feature 'Favorites' (or 'Favourites' on the British version of AOL).

**bounce** An email message returned to the sender because it was sent to an invalid address.

**bps** Bits per second. See bit.

**browser** Special software that you need to view a web page and navigate the web. The two main browsers are Netscape Navigator and Microsoft Internet Explorer.

**certificate** A unique set of numbers that has been generated by a trusted company (such as VeriSign or Thawte) – but only once they are satisfied that the company is legitimate and authentic. The company can now use this certificate to provide authentication (that it is who and what it claims to be) and set up a secure website to accept payments online.

**CGI Common Gateway Interface.** An advanced feature of website programming that allows a web page to send information to a program running on the server. For example, if a web page has a search feature, the search term you enter on the web page is sent to the search program using CGI. See also Perl.

**click through** A measure used with banner ads to charge the advertiser for the advert. Each time a surfer clicks on a displayed ad (that links to the advertiser's main site), the advertiser is charged a fee. A click through rate of just a few percent is common and most advertisers have to pay per thousand impressions of their banner ad.

**cookie** A tiny scrap of information stored on your computer by a website. Sounds very much like Big Brother, but it's usually used by shops to store information about when you last visited the shop, your last order number or account number. Normally totally harmless and sometimes necessary for a shopping site to work at all.

**CPA Cost Per Action**. The cost of one impression of a banner ad.

**CTR Click Through Rate.** The cost of one click through on a banner ad.

**database** A way of organising your information so that it is stored in a uniform way and can be published on your website – allowing visitors to search and view the information: for example, your company's catalogue of products, a telephone directory or an encyclopaedia of terms. To publish a complex database, you'll need to talk to your website provider and either use a commercial product or a custom-written program written in the Perl programming language.

**digital certificate** See certificate.

**directory** A website that contains a list of other websites, normally organised into sections and often with a search feature. Yahoo! (**www. yahoo.co.uk**) is one of the best-known directories and lists half a million websites.

**domain name** The unique name that identifies one site or server on the Internet. For example, the domain name 'microsoft.com' identifies the server provided by Microsoft.

**DNS Domain Name System.** A method of converting the domain name to the IP (Internet protocol) address (a series of numbers) that's actually used to locate the computer. The list of names and addresses are stored on a domain-name server (also called DNS). For example, if you type in the domain name 'www.microsoft.com' in your web browser, this is passed to a DNS that translates the name to a set of numbers that points to the Microsoft server.

**download** To transfer a file from a distant computer on to your own, via the Internet.

**encryption** A way of scrambling a piece of text so that only the intended recipient can read it.

**e-wallet** Feature of new web browsers that lets you enter a range of different ways of paying for your shopping. You might include your credit card and e-cash, then open your e-wallet when you visit a shop. It's one future method of managing spending on the net.

**FAQ Frequently Asked Question.** Some websites allow you to click on this and then present you with some commonly asked questions and their answers.

**firewall** Special security system (normally installed in a company) that lets users in the company access the Internet but prevents outside hackers gaining access to the company's computers. If your company has a firewall installed, it can prevent you from accessing a secure website (such as a shop or bank account).

**flame** To receive rude messages in response to a posting on a discussion group or newsgroup; generally this happens if you post a provocative, stupid or overtly commercial message.

**folder** In an email program, this refers to a container for your email messages or, on a hard disk, it's a container for files.

**forward** Feature of email software that lets you send a message you've received on to another user.

**freeware** Software that can be used on a permanent basis without charge.

**FTP File Transfer Protocol.** Protocol used to transfer files between computers over the Internet.

**gateway** A link between two different systems. For example, an email gateway can be used to resend an email message to a fax machine or pager.

**geotargeting** Method of analysing what a visitor to your website is viewing or doing and deducing their location, then displaying custom content or advertisements accordingly; for example, if they ask for the weather in Seattle, you could display adverts from taxi companies in Seattle.

**GIF** A common graphics format used to store images on a web page.

**hit** A request from a user's browser to view a page or image on your website. Often misleadingly used as a measure of the popularity of a website or a measure of the number of visitors – it will not provide any of this information: you'll need to analyse your site's access log files to find these details. The problem occurs because as each element within a web page is displayed, it generates a 'hit'. If your home page has three pictures and some text, every user will generate four hits in your access log.

**home page** The first page you see when you visit a website. The home page is normally stored in a file called 'index.html'. If you visit 'www.microsoft.com' you are actually viewing the Microsoft home page on its website.

**HTML HyperText Markup Language.** The set of codes that are used to lay out and format a web page. These codes let you add links, change text to bold, use colours and insert images into a page.

**HTTP HyperText Transfer Protocol.** The series of commands (protocol) used by a web browser to ask an Internet server for a particular web page. You'll see this at the start of most web addresses (though you don't have to type it in) to identify this address as a web page rather than a file (which uses a sister protocol, FTP).

**hypertext** A way of connecting web pages together across the web. One word or image in a page can be linked (this facility is often called a hyperlink) to any other page on the site or on any other site on the web. When the user clicks on the link, they jump immediately to the referenced page. It's the way you browse and surf the web.

**IE Internet Explorer.** Microsoft's web browser software.

**impression** The act of displaying a banner ad to a visitor. This is normally used as a way of charging the advertiser for their banner ad – for example, you might be charged £140 ($200) per thousand impressions shown on a random basis. This means that the website has several banner ads and will rotate them on a random basis, charging each advertiser £140 ($200) every thousandth time their advert is displayed.

**Internet or net** The millions of computers that are linked together around the world so that each can communicate with others. The Internet is public, so any user can visit any other computer linked to the Internet.

**intranet** A mini, private Internet within a company. Employees can browse their company information in just the same way as you would on an Internet using a web browser.

**ISDN Integrated Services Digital Network.** A high-speed digital version of your standard old phone line. You'll get a speedy connection to the Internet using an ISDN link, but you need a special modem (called a Terminal Adapter) and an ISP that provides ISDN access for its users. ISDN, however, is being overtaken by the new cable modem and ADSL technology.

**ISP Internet Service Provider.** A company that provides a doorway on to the Internet for you, the user.

**JavaScript** Special programming language that lets web-page designers enhance the basic effects provided by HTML.

**keyword** A word that you type into a search engine to find information.

**link** See hypertext.

**Listserv** See mailing list.

**logfile** See access log.

**mailbox** Special area at your ISP where your incoming mail messages are temporarily stored until you connect to the net and download and read the mail.

**mailing list** Way of distributing messages, thoughts or news to a group of users. It's a collection of email addresses stored on a special computer to form a special group of users interested in a particular subject. Any message sent to the mailing list computer is automatically redistributed to all the users on the list.

**mail server** A computer on the Internet that deals with your email: storing your incoming mail until you log in and read it, and passing on the email messages you send to the right address. Your ISP will provide you with the addresses of its mail server. You may need to configure your email software to look at this address for your new mail.

**modem** A special device that connects your computer to a telephone line and allows you to dial and connect to an ISP – and so gain access to the Internet (the word comes from 'modulator' and 'demodulator'). A modem works by converting your computer's data into sound signals that can be sent along a phone line. New communication systems (like ISDN, ADSL and cable modems) do away with this conversion and send information in its native digital format to provide much higher transfer speeds.

**name server** A special computer on the Internet that converts a domain name to its IP address. See DNS.

**newsgroup** There are 60,000 newsgroups on the net and collectively these are called the Usenet. Each newsgroup is a discussion forum about a particular subject, hobby or interest. You'll need a newsgroup reader, which is part of your web browser, to read and submit messages.

**newsreader** Special software you need to access, read and post messages to a newsgroup – both web browsers from Microsoft and Netscape have a newsreader built in.

**offline** Not connected to the Internet.

**online** Connected to the Internet, so incurring telephone charges.

**opt-in mailing list** List of email addresses in which each recipient has specifically asked to receive advertising email messages – normally so that they can keep up to date with a topic or industry. If you buy an email mailing list, make sure that it's an opt-in list.

**page impression** A measure that's used to count how many times a web page has been displayed to a visitor to a website. Normally used as a crude counter for the number of visitors to a site and not as realistic as analysis of your website's access log. See also impression.

**page requests** A measure of the number of pages viewed in a day, providing an indication of the popularity of your website. For a true indication, you should use special software to analyse your site's access logs and count the number of individual visitors – after all, a visitor might view several pages.

**Perl** If you visit a website that implements a shopping cart, quiz or response form, there's a fair chance that it' been created using the Perl programming language; it's hard to master, but dominant in the webbed world – for more details try the official Perl site (**www.perl.org**).

**PGP Pretty Good Privacy.** A way of encrypting an email (or file) so that only the intended recipient can decrypt and read the message – used by some small shopping sites to let customers send in their credit card details.

**plug-in** Special program that works in conjunction with your web browser to provide an extra feature (often multimedia, video or animation) – if you need a plug-in to view a particular web page, you'll be told and given the chance to download the file automatically.

**PoP Point of Presence.** A telephone number (provided by your ISP) that your modem dials to connect to their computer and so to the Internet. Make sure that your ISP provides PoPs in your local area and that these are either local phone numbers or special numbers that are charged at the same rate as a local number (called lo-call numbers, these often start with the code 0345 or 0845).

**privacy statement** Company policy published on your website that explains to visitors and customers what you will (and preferably will not) do with their personal details – such as their email address. Used to reassure customers that you're not about to resell their details as a mailing list.

**protocol** A set of rules that define the way something happens. For example, the POP3 system of sending mail is a protocol that defines the commands used to actually transfer the message.

**public domain** Something (either a text or program) that is freely available to anyone to view or try. The copyright remains with the original author, so you can't copy it, resell it or change it without their permission.

**restocking** fee Some shopping sites will accept returned goods only on condition that you pay a fee. Avoid these sites.

**secure site** A shopping site that provides a system (almost always the SSL standard) to ensure that there is a secure channel between the site and your browser – anything you type in (such as your credit card details) cannot be unscrambled or read by a hacker.

**server access logs** See access log.

**SET Secure Electronic Transmission.** Secure method of paying for goods over the net; a more secure alternative to typing in your credit card details – instead, your browser provides your unique identification code to a shop, which it then passes on to a bank.

**shopping cart/basket** An electronic equivalent of the wire basket or trolley you use in your supermarket. Lets you add items as you browse a shopping site, then move to the checkout to pay.

**signature** (1) A unique code that identifies a person or company – often used to prove the authenticity of a secure website. (2) A few lines of text that are automatically added to any email you write or newsgroup message that you post. Your signature could just include your name or provide contact details or company name and slogan.

**smiley** A facial expression made up of keyboard characters, often added to email or newsgroup postings to add expression or feeling. For example :-) means happy, funny or a joke.

**snail mail** The old-fashioned method of sending a letter via the Post Office.

**spam** Unwanted email – normally sent in bulk to advertise something.

**SSL Secure Sockets Layer.** A way of scrambling the data between your web browser and the website so that no hacker or eavesdropper can read the information you are sending. Normally used on a web page that asks you to enter a credit card number or personal details. Your browser will indicate a secure SSL page by displaying a tiny closed padlock icon in the bottom line of the window. Don't shop without this!

**TCP/IP Transmission Control Protocol/Internet Protocol.** The rules that describe how all information is sent over the Internet and how it finds its way to the right destination.

**Telnet** Special program that lets you connect to any computer on the Internet and type in commands as if you were sitting in front of the computer's keyboard. In practice, you'll use Telnet only for advanced website management – to move files around your website and change options.

**UART Universal Asynchronous Receiver/Transmitter.** A special chip in your computer responsible for sending and receiving data in a serial form – that means anything sent via a modem.

**unsolicited mail** An advertising email message that has not been requested. Often called 'spam' email. Don't send out unsolicited mail to unknown email addresses unless you want to annoy the recipients and damage your company's reputation.

**URL Uniform Resource Locator.** The correct name for the full address of a web page. For example, 'microsoft.com' is a domain name, 'www.microsoft.com' is the website address for Microsoft and 'www.microsoft.com/index.html' is the URL to the site's home page.

**Usenet** The collective name for the mass of over 60,000 newsgroups on the Internet.

**Uuencoding** An older method of converting files into a special format before attaching them to an email message. Thankfully, you don't need to do this any more owing to the arrival of MIME (Multipurpose Internet Multimedia Extensions), which automatically sorts out attachments.

**web browser** A software program that lets you view a web page and navigate around the web.

**web page** A single, individual page within a website. Each web page is stored in a separate file; the file contains HTML commands that describe the text, its layout, formatting and links.

**web server** A computer that stores a website (generally, web servers store hundreds of separate websites or, in the case of mammoth sites from the BBC or CNN, the website is big enough to deserve its own web server).

**website** A collection of web pages produced by one person or company and about a particular subject.

**WWW World Wide Web or W3 or web.** The collective name for the millions of individual websites on the Internet.

**Winsock** Software that lets your computer communicate with the Internet via a standard dial-up connection; Windows includes a Winsock utility and it's configured automatically – you shouldn't need to do anything!

# //INDEX

## //A

accepting payment, 46
access logs, 77
accountants (www sites), 114
   international (www sites), 116
accounts (www sites), 112
   accounting software (www sites), 116
address, website, 25
advertising, 65
   advertising agencies, 72, 217
   banner advertising, 65, 71
advice, business (www sites), 119
anti-virus, 22

## //B

banking (www sites), 156
bankruptcy (www sites), 160
banner advertising, 65, 71
   costs, 66
   standard sizes, 66
brand promotion, 68
browsers. See web browser
browsing (FAQs), 227
building a website. See website design
business
   advice (www sites), 119
   banking (www sites), 156
   business portals, 109
   business websites, 30
   buying or selling (www sites), 126
   discussion online, 94
   finding a business, 82
   global. See export
   magazines (www sites), 203
   news (www sites), 199
   newsgroups, 105
   online, 5
   plans (www sites), 126
   starting up (www sites), 125
   websites, 23
Business to Business (www sites), 133
buying or selling a business
(www sites), 126

## //C

cars and vans (www sites), 144
cash, 59
chat
   FAQs, 230
   grouhd rules, 100
commercial property (www sites), 145
company research (www sites), 210
computer
   equipment (www sites), 148
   support (www sites), 149
confidentiality, 17
consumer complaints, 59
content (website), 30
credit card
   authorising, 47
   credit cards (www sites), 166
   processing bureaux, 57

## //D

database, 38
databases online, 33

Also published in the Virgin Internet Guide series...

**The Virgin Guide to the Internet**
The advice you need to plug in, log on and get going.

**The Virgin Family Internet Guide**
The only book that lets your family get the best out of the Internet
– and lock out the worst.

**The Virgin Internet Shopping Guide**
You can now buy almost anything on the Internet, and this book
shows you how.

**The Virgin Internet Travel Guide**
The complete guide to choosing your destination
– and getting the best deal online.

**The Virgin Internet Money Guide**
Get your personal finances sorted – online.

**The Virgin Internet Music Guide**
The web is alive – with the sound of music.

Forthcoming titles:

**The Virgin Internet Research Guide**
How to find out just about anything on the net.

**The Virgin Weird Internet Guide**
Strange and wonderful places to surf.

**The Virgin Internet Auction Guide**
Bid for a bargain.

For more information, ask your friendly local bookseller – or check
out our website: **http://www.virginbooks.com**